Lynne Palmer's

$20.00

THE NEXT FOUR YEARS

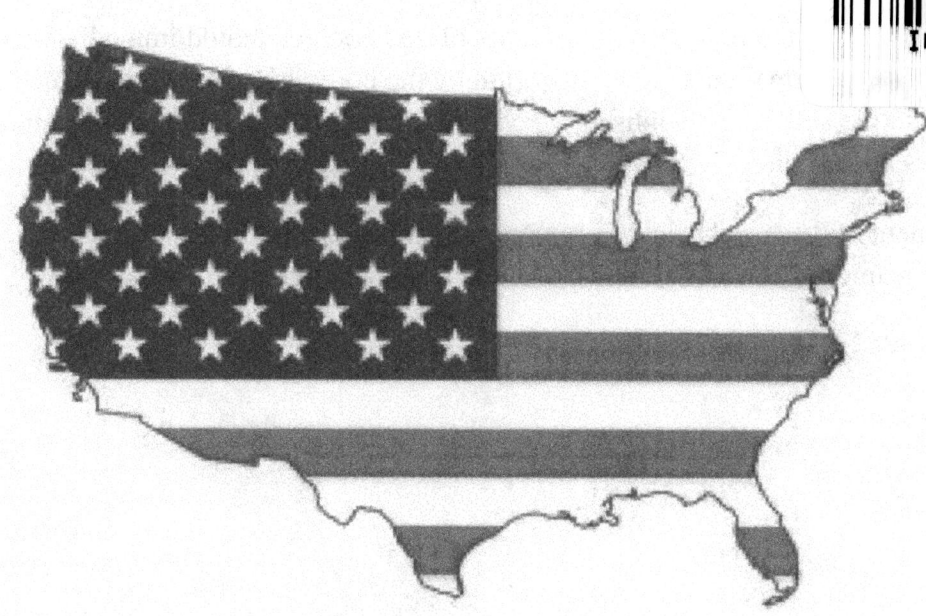

THE HOROSCOPES OF THE USA & PRESIDENT OBAMA

How Your Life Could Be Affected

COPYRIGHT © 2012 BY LYNNE PALMER

All rights reserved worldwide. This is copyrighted material. No part of this booklet may be used or reproduced in any form or by any electronic or mechanical means, including, but not limited to, information storage or retrieval systems, without permission in writing from **Lynne Palmer.**

Anyone being requested to reproduce all or parts of this booklet should immediately contact the publisher to verify information and authorization by the copyright owner and to receive written permission from the author and publisher, except in the case of brief quotations embodied in critical reviews and articles.

Any infringement of these rights and/or removal of any copyright notices by publishers, printers, marketing companies or others will be prosecuted to the full extent of the law.

ISBN#: 978-0-9827458-5-4

TABLE OF CONTENTS

Introduction	4
Chart: The Horoscope of the USA	6
Money and The Economy	7
Employment	24
The Stock Market	32
Real Estate, Property and Housing	39
Crime, Spies, Terrorists and Place of Confinement	42
War, International Disputes and Foreign Nations	48
Transportation	53
Education, Communication and the Media	61
Entertainment	65
Chart: President Barack Obama	71
The Horoscope of President Barack Obama	72

INTRODUCTION

Those who have never been to an astrologer or read any technical books on the subject are not aware that a horoscope of a country can be charted astrologically. This is called Mundane Astrology.

The Horoscope of the United States of America is based upon when the USA became independent, which was July 4, 1776. It is cast for Philadelphia, Pennsylvania (74W08, 39N57) for a rectified time of 2h14'15" am local mean time. The chart in this Special Report is the one employed by C.C. Zain, which I have found to be quite accurate. Therefore the present and future planetary aspects that are delineated in this report are based on this information.

How Does Astrology Work?

A Horoscope consists of 12 Zodiac signs and 10 Planets (including the Sun and Moon, which are luminaries, but for simplification, astrologers call them planets) and 12 Houses (each house represents a different department of life). The 10 planets and 12 houses fall into these areas and indicate the basic characteristics of a nation, depending upon the aspects formed by the planets.

Each sign and planet radiates a particular kind of energy which corresponds to its own nature; this energy is expressed on either the positive or negative side. The harmonious aspects bring the easy things often called luck; good fortune is attracted when you use the harmonious side of a sign and/or planet. The inharmonious aspects bring the struggles and obstacles often involved with losses and/or problems; misfortune or difficulties occur when you use the inharmonious side of a sign and/or planet.

You will notice, by reading these pages, that there are overlapping and conflicting dates and events because there are favorable and unfavorable aspects in simultaneously. The USA Horoscope may affect each individual in a different way. For example: the weather may be bad in one part of the country, thus destroying property and the home a person lives in. However, in another state, the weather does not upset individual lives. Some people play the stock market and do well. Others lose when investing. Your own horoscope will indicate conditions favorable for winning, or unfavorable conditions which cause a loss. Therefore, everyone is affected differently. During the Great Depression there were those who lost everything, while others became rich. By knowing how the economy of the USA is during a specific time, and all of the other areas mentioned in this report, you can plan your life accordingly. Positive thinking and having faith that you and the nation will pull through is half the battle. There will be periods of ease, joy and happiness as well as the dark periods. However, your attitude and reaction is of utmost importance. The American people can prosper even when times are rough. According to the USA Horoscope, the American people will always be saved monetarily. The two luckiest planets in Astrology are in the money house of the United States Horoscope.

The Horoscope of President Barack Obama indicates that he is the person needed for this country. His harmonious aspects, when he puts them to use, will benefit the USA. The saying, "Everything happens for the best" is an attitude that is positive, especially when you compare his chart with that of the USA. He brings luck to the United States of America. People need patience to see the results.

The USA Horoscope indicates that the world is not coming to an end. We experience catastrophes such as when the entire world is plugged into gigantic conflicts which could lead to war, or just international disputes. However, terrorists, earthquakes, floods, hurricanes and other disasters may continue. Thus, a worldwide cooperative effort for the good of the universe is needed.

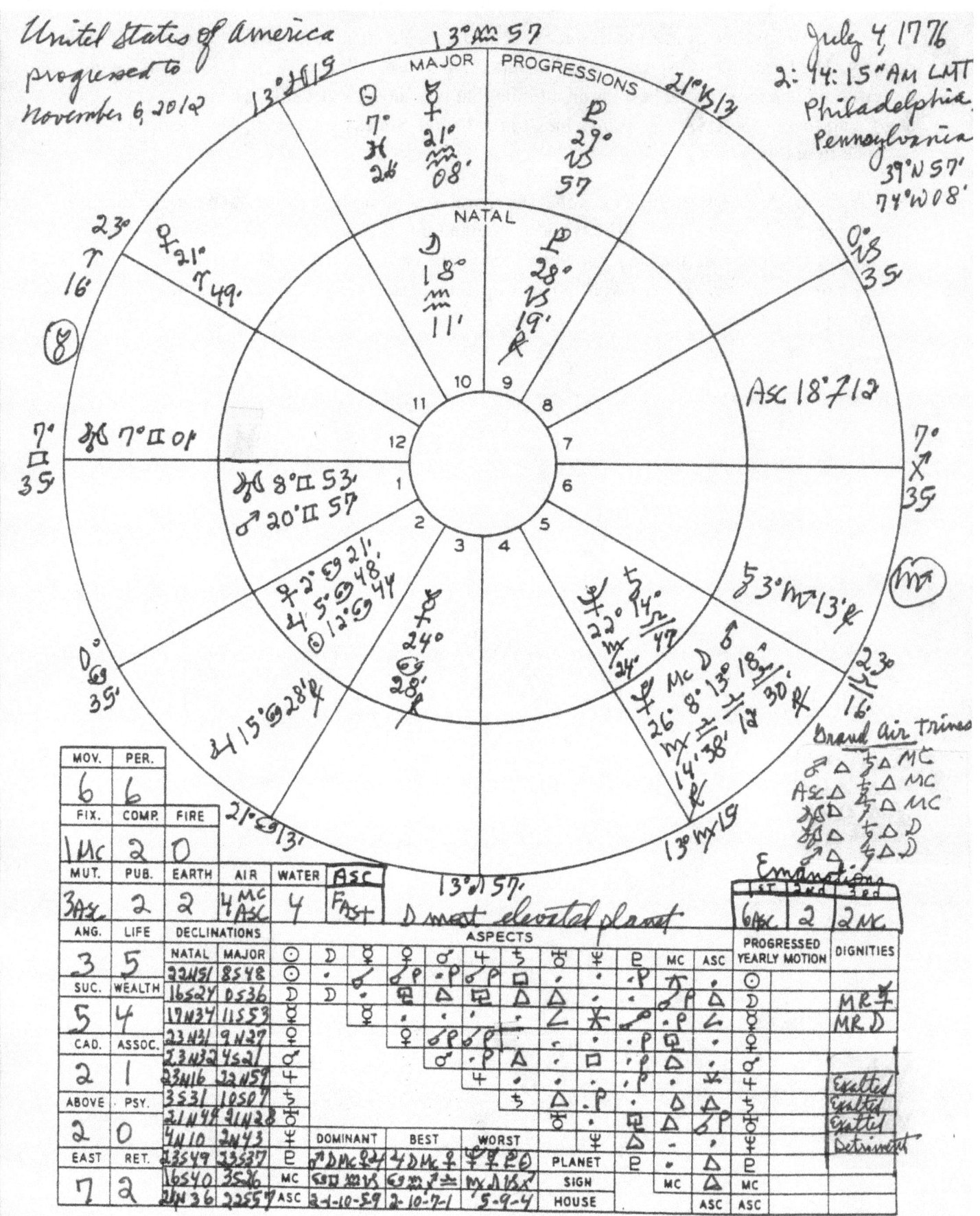

THE HOROSCOPE OF THE USA

MONEY AND THE ECONOMY

In to March 11, 2014

One moment people worry about the economy and their money-making opportunities, the next moment they tend to spend. People spend money on beauty products (men and women both buy perfume, get facials) and buy clothes – many want to be well groomed when they attend social events, and go to night clubs. They spend money fast on these items; also, money is made by Americans who are in these fields. Income is slightly boosted.

Bargains are attracted. Lower prices for goods and food boost the economy. Those companies and businesses who deal in the necessities are favored to do well. Loans, with low interest rates, could help people get out of debt.

****

In to October 22, 2033

The economy appears to be slowly recovering; commerce improves somewhat; the economy could get a slight lift. The debts due from foreign nations could be paid in small amounts over a period of time. A tax cut could help improve the economy; however, problems still prevail with the National debt. An improvement in social security, Medicare, pensions, health care and insurance programs could be in the news. The American people may try to use caution and may avoid spending on fun, entertainment and luxuries.

Those rich citizens who were born wealthy and have "old" money are more conservative than those who suddenly make a fortune. Art is a form of investment that is very popular with the conservative types; they also hold on to their money invested in stocks and gold. Many people will spend money on art and collectibles as a hedge against inflation.

There is a beneficial financial period; however, it is not that noticeable because all the bad aspects outweigh the good, therefore, the following will be experienced by some people – those that have a good head on their shoulder, are grounded, practical and do not worry or cry the blues. There are those who are easily depressed and negative that will tune in easier to discord than harmony. These are the people who will notice the favorable times, but will mainly dwell on the unfavorable times. Therefore, those who are sound, calm, serious and well-balanced, lower prices and reduced taxes show that the country is being stabilized. Old ways could be put back into use; the effect of those things which stood the trials of time makes the citizens of the United States reassured that things are improving.

Many people are focused on purchasing collectibles as a hedge against inflation. They put themselves on a budget: they'll look for sales and attend flea markets and could wind up with valuable items. The lottery and other forms of gambling are popular and aid many people in their search for wealth. The tax revenues from casinos, and the state, help boost the economy. The gambler who is cool-headed does the best, whereas those who have gambling fever and take risks do not fare so well.

Many Americans find it easier to pay their taxes, especially since the Internal Revenue Service works with the people by putting them on a better installment plan than the treasury had in bygone years.

The dollar could improve overseas due to the US currency being up; thus people may make plans to travel aboard. The skies seem safe; planes and airports could be well guarded. International travel is on the rise. Tourism is big business overseas; American's spend lots of money traveling and purchasing items, even if they are highly priced. However, when there's a slow economy many people will stay home. But those who are rich will travel aboard and spend their dollars freely.

Many Americans make steady, financial plans for their future and the future of their children. Some schools and playgrounds are free from harm.

****

In to May 3, 2014 to March 29, 2015

Even though many areas are improving and looking good, there are aspects that cause issues for many. There are obstacles with the people's money – lots of confusion, "Should I spend money or not? Will I have a job? Should I chance going on a spending spree?" It is the news media that causes the public to be perplexed – bad press messes with the thoughts of the populace.

Many people, who have money saved, will want to travel by rail, car or bus; perhaps, take a short distance journey to Mexico, Canada, or someplace near to their home. But they are hesitant to spend their money on such luxuries as a vacation or a visit to relatives. Americans may want to buy a new communication system, but with a shaky economy they could make do with what they have. If they do buy something, the news coverage may be that it's on recall because something is wrong with it.

Americans spend money on books, education, communication devices, travel, art, beauty, fashion, jewelry, parties and entertainment. Society people are in the news; their galas, banquets, jewels, furs and designer clothes cost them plenty and are reported by the press. However, these same people may be confused in monetary issues. Should they buy art, give expensive parties, spend money on luxury goods or go to a fancy restaurant? When some of them continue their lavish lifestyles, some members of the press, and the common classes of people, might put them down, because the economy is suffering.

In to January 13, 2013 and from October 24, 2013 to September 18, 2014

Radical activities could receive lots of publicity. Citizens of the USA want something new to happen that will bring in money. Many will be fired or laid off and in a state of shock at these sudden events that transpire which can also be with the President and the Administration as well as banks and the Treasury. Controversy from the current regime upsets the public. The American people will criticize President Obama and his staff. Many of his staff will resign or be changed. The consumer is erratic, unpredictable and wants to take rebellious action against those in power. People are upset about their money and jobs. Computers, electronics, cars and new ways of doing things are on the agenda. However, due to the unusual ways of Americans, they could wind up spending money erratically on these and other items – and later, wish they had done differently.

There are many who rebel for change. Others will be calm, cool and think twice about getting involved in radical action. It seems that life is topsy-turvy at this time for the radicals. There may be many upheavals in the art world-like the price of paintings. Cosmetic and beauty products may cost more. These radicals tend to be involved in a desire to break the rules because they desire radical change. The press will have a field day with everything that takes place.

****

In to November 16, 2015

The time when the forming of one group (or more) accomplishes some purpose, which will benefit the masses. These groups, and their activities, help our finances and society in general. They are for the right of the universe.

Generous sums of money are donated by the American people to hospitals and charitable causes. Society people will spend lavishly on galas, benefits, and the arts. Schools donate to the needy. Movie stars and celebrities give to charitable causes. For example: the humanitarian aid we give in goods that help the refugees and those who are needy.

****

In Now and for the Upcoming Years

Donations to charitable causes may be on the increase due to the efforts of those in society who give galas, banquets and parties that attract the affluent. Art flourishes; lots of money is spent by the people who collect sculpture and fine paintings.

Congress brings luck to the general populace by allotting financial aid to those who are unemployed. Many Civil service employees could receive financial aid through Congress. Congress will aid hospitals and the unemployed.

Luxury items are bought by those who can afford them. Money is earned by the Americans, when they have jobs that cater to these expensive items: beauty salons, spas where people are pampered, five-star restaurants and hotels, galas, art gallery parties, designer clothes, homes and furnishings that cost a fortune (their servants earn plenty). The Members of Congress and our ambassadors to foreign nations hob-knob with this society-political element. However, criticism can be expected up to October 2, 2018, when the current regime and the wealth mix and mingle – especially when it costs so much money to entertain and be entertained.

****

In to August 3, 2013

The finances of the people are not improved as much as the public and administration hopes for. United States citizens have lots of faith that their finances will improve considerably. But, unfortunately, that's not the case.

Lots of money is spent on the War Effort. US War bonds could be a popular form of investment; the administration could encourage people to buy them – they can benefit the government and in the long run be an asset to those who purchase them.

An enormous amount of money may be spent on American embassies and Ambassadors who reside overseas. They do favors, and spread good will to other nations; thus, this exorbitant show-off of extravagance reflects favorably on the credit, prestige and reputation of the USA. The United States' allies may go out of their way to help us, even though it is at a huge expense to America. Congress and the administration could believe this wanton spending of money is the way to go. It pays off a lot, but not as much as expected; however, because of it there are many favorable financial transactions between the USA and foreign nations.

The amount of funds in banks, the National Treasury and the public's personal bank accounts could be on the rise. However, people should exercise caution and not get too carried away with spending sprees.

Non-speculative bonds and securities could cost plenty, and return a slight increase – but again people should be careful of being overly confident when it comes to monetary concerns. Even Congress and the administration are sure the economy will pick up – it will, but not as much as the government expects.

Capitalism flourishes. Citizens of the USA can be extravagant, pay too high a price for goods; they're overconfident and struggle to pay higher prices, which is the price of war.

Prices for goods go sky-high. Money spent on the education of children, schools and colleges is exorbitant, especially that allotted by Congress. Postal prices increase as well as telephone bills. Cell phones, faxes and land phone systems are overloaded, thus people pay more for using them. There are important developments in transportation and the communication fields; thus, prices spiral. Americans could overspend in all of the communication areas – we like to talk and keep in touch with others. Inflation continues.

In to July 22, 2018

There is a gradual increase in USA citizens' bank accounts, and those confident and wealthy classes will pull through any financial problems that arise. Money, and great riches, gradually earns these people more and more money as time goes by. So, does their expenditures. Somehow, Americans, for the most part, get saved. For years, there are increases, then decreases, with the money and personal possessions of the people. The National Treasury and banks are part of this up and down trend. Its feast or famine; inflation or recession.

****

In Now and for the Upcoming Years

Money increases from interstate and international commerce and traffic, foreign shipping by large corporations, radio and television areas, advertising and publishing, some aid for teachers, churches, and satellites in space – some of the public is cooperative with the current regime. Tariffs from other nations can boost the economy. Fund-raising to help the needy is beneficial for the USA. The United Nations, NATO and other groups involved on committees and meeting to discuss nuclear and economic issues can impress the public and be favorable for the increase of money coming into the United States.

Congress takes quick action to allot money for military spending and special operations overseas (The Delta Force, Navy Seals, Green Berets, Rangers) and for those who guard our nation at home (policemen, sheriffs, sky marshals, National Guard and Homeland Security).

Military spending and activity is likely to be stepped up; danger of the war expanding against terrorists is a slow process. Lavish expenditures by Congress for the war effort; many Americans may argue not to spend so much money. Cooperative humanitarian efforts to relieve the suffering of large masses of people overseas (like the refugees) are undertaken.

People spend plenty on liquor. Prices of manufactured goods are on the increase. Entertainment and sport tickets are costly when prices rise in these areas. However, optimistic and risk-taking Americans will gladly pay the price for fun and pleasure.

****

In Now and for the Upcoming Years

There's a gradual slow down in the American market in regards to oil production. The oil in various states (Texas, Oklahoma) is not fully utilized due to the government's need to appease the Arab oil-producing countries. As time goes by, our gas and oil supply could lessen and we could have an oil shortage.

Congress and the administration may promise a tax cut to help the American people; some relief may come but it may not be enough – thus, this causes people to be disappointed but at the same time it puts a drain on the USA's money supply.

Congress could gradually continue to impose more taxes on the tobacco industry. Class action court cases are heard from people, who came down with lung cancer, or their relatives bring suit, these suits and an increase of taxes could cost the tobacco industry enormous losses if a life was lost.

Members of Congress could be divided when it comes to the salary cuts of government workers. Congress may be indecisive about revoking, repealing or acting upon legislative measures during this time. When decisions are made, it could be too long in coming; therefore, the economy does not get the boost it sorely needs; however, some favorable aspects could somewhat offset the financial problems of the nation.

However, there could be postponements to take action because they are unsure of which way to move on this problem. Instead, they may impose tariffs on imported goods, but that may not boost the economy as much as needed.

Congress and the administration are likely to look through rose colored glasses when dealing with poor nations; thus, they could grant them loans which may never be paid back.

Foreign nations, especially Third World countries, are slow in paying their debt to the USA; thus making money tight for Americans. There's a further deficit in the budget, if the government loans money to other countries.

Furthermore, demands for our tax money from third world nations in disaster situations, puts a large drain on our finances, especially when these countries can't repay their debt to us. It's a mistake; they show poor judgment and could put citizens of the USA into a financial panic or slump.

Cruise ships attract money losses when the economy is on the decline. Congress could promise to bail them out, but delays or postponements could make matters worse.

Some financial areas improve slowly; thus, many will earn money but will be careful and practical. Then there are the big-time spendthrifts who will go on sprees as fast as their dollars roll in. When the bad economical times come, such as a recession, many Americans get saved at the last minute. Congress may not act fast enough to help trade people; thus, many may declare bankruptcy. However, if the employer has a worker take a cut a pay, the laborer has to economize even further than before. People may be slow in paying taxes, especially foreign nations who are in debt to the United States. Many tend to be ultra-conservative and cut down on costs, and eliminate waste, and spend only on the bare necessities, or on inexpensive items.

The economy is affected by a slowing down period. People worry about losses, security, and money. Many people are unemployed due to scarcity of jobs, which in turn brings a demand on the part of labor. Laborers want the minimum wage raised; however, the National Debt may be such that this is delayed.

People may worry about laws being passed which could cause them to have reduced checks, or health care. This type of action, reported by the press, has the senior citizens nervous and confused. Many Americans will become depressed over the news coverage, loss of work, or loss of a home due to foreclosure – real estate losses occur when people can't meet their obligation.

Measures of protection can be taken to protect assets, homes, lands, and money – but they may not come as fast as people need, or want.

Americans are confused about any improvement coming, especially when they learn through the press that the National Debt is high. More protection could put a drain on the economy and National Budget during this time. Panic states can be reached if the citizens of the USA are told conflicting reports by an administration which is evasive, or the press reporting things as worse than they really are.

People are worried that their dollars could be devalued or fall low in comparison to the world currency market. Money can be tight, thus, the USA's trade business with others could be affected. There can be a slowing down process with the US economy. The unemployment rate could be at an all-time high; job cuts, reduction of salaries – the people's money is at a low ebb. Many rules, regulations and benefits such as pensions, IRA's and tax deferred annuities help the working class.

If the USA's taxes are lowered, it may help some people, temporarily, but it puts an enormous burden on the low money supply. But it could cost the government more than they could afford during this time; however, if the administration obliges the public, the National Debt becomes quite heavy.

Debts due from other nations could be postponed or not aid at all – that increases economy problems. If the United States reduces the tariffs from international commerce and trade, the USA loses a lot of revenue money; thus putting a strain on the National Treasury. This added tariff money is sorely needed, and could be a boost to America.

Furthermore, demands for our tax money from third world nations in disaster situations, puts a large drain on our finances, especially when these countries can't repay their debt to us. Congress and the administration are likely to look through rose colored glasses when dealing with poor nations, thus, they could grant them loans which may never be paid back.

International flights could have heavy tariffs on the airports; thus, tickets may be high – but it is for safety reasons that there is an increase in security measures. People who do travel may think that security is not tight enough. That type of news adds more fear to those who fly.

People could be cautious with credit card spending; they've learned from their past mistakes. Americans are interested in saving money so they will have something to fall back upon if times get rough.

Americans may be so heavily in debt that they are unable to pay the money they owe to financial institutions – loans and credit cards. Furthermore, the banks may not loan them anymore money, especially when their income is reduced, because people fail to pay their obligation. Thus, the banks lose money.

The government could impose rules and restrictions upon people so they'll be conservative, especially with water, and take too long, if at all, to enact laws which could benefit the country and its people. If Congress finally decides to pass a law there could be so many restrictions placed upon it that it doesn't help the economy.

Unemployment checks may be delayed or lost, or mistakes made by those whose job it is due to administer them. The public could be confused and think that their money isn't going to arrive, because the government is broke. Old-age pensions, Medicare, and social security could be lowered, or problems with them are in the news.

Insurance companies may experience delays in collecting money paid to them for insurance coverage. Pay outs from the insurance company to the insured could be delayed or tied up in the courts. Homes damaged by storms, hurricanes, tornadoes, or earthquakes could be uninsured; if insured, the people who put in an insurance claim may have to wait awhile to collect the insurance money due them. Money problems abound for insurance companies.

****

In to February 9, 2026

Manufacture companies may worry. There will gradually be an increase of more people investing in the USA's industrial field. Loans could aid these businesses, people can be employed – it just does not happen overnight. It is a slow building up in manufacturing. Companies in foreign nations could open up their companies in the USA, thus employing many Americans and helping the economy.

There are up and down money and economy problems for years. But keep in mind – the USA will always manage to be saved, although at moments it may not seem possible. People need to have faith (and some do) --- Patience is needed.

****

April 24, 2013 to April 23, 2014

Lots of shocks from the President, and those in high positions, regarding the banks, National Treasury and the public's money. Upheavals and topsy-turvy conditions prevail – the press reports erratic changes, unpredictable actions by politicians and revolutionary protests by the American people. Secret deals and negotiations behind closed doors are leaked and this sudden and unexpected news could cause upheavals. The general populace may cry out for the President to step down and terminate his position, especially when his ideas for change create controversy and rebellion. The public, President, legislators, and congressional representatives are all at odds with each other – the radicals are in the news. An exposé could shock the nation and damage considerably the reputation and business outlook of the USA in world affairs. Chaos and a marked change from old conditions to new ones cause uproar – the press reports one shock and exposé after another.

This a very bad time for the President, and his staff to initiate anything new, different or innovative. The majority of these people will not tolerate this action – many of the protesters will be arrested and that will keep the press busy – the headlines spread rumors like wildfire. The media fails to report everything and the administration could make mistakes that are covered up. The President tries to encourage people not get upset over the economy and his new ideas for reform. This is a time when people need to be calm, analytical, and practical and know that the USA is somehow going to pull through all of these shocking upheavals and radical changes that cannot be kept secret.

This is an extremely rough time for the economy with sudden, unexpected, and unpredictable changes. Lots of shocks from the government regarding the banks, National Treasury, minting of coins, non-speculative bonds and securities, gold and money in general. Upheavals and topsy-turvy conditions prevail. Everyone is erratic. Secret deals are made by the administration; however, leaks bring exposés of those in high places.

There could be public outcry of the administration by the people and the press, due to conflicting reports about the banks, the National Treasury, non-speculative bonds and securities, the personal property of the people (their money, possessions, source of income, lands and homes) and what the government intends to do to solve America's financial crisis.

Frustrations over money. The administration does not have much control over these issues. Those in authority throw their weight around in trying to help the people's money. A lot of money could be spent on the White House, embassies and homes of the people. Our economy could be threatened anew by gold. Gold is in the headlines.

Is Fort Knox safe from terrorists? It is known to be heavily guarded. But our gold supply could be discussed.

The countries overseas will be astounded over the sudden, unexpected and unpredictable changes of affairs in the US by these radicals who are causing all sorts of problems (including monetary). Exposés of the administration turns everything upside down. Meetings are cancelled. Monetary issues over the National Treasury throw things asunder. All of these activities are reported by the media.

Business is affected by the entire controversy taking place. It damages the credit, honor and reputation of the United States. Our influence in world affairs is down. However, the USA has other very favorable aspects that can pull us out of this mess. Other nations, especially our allies, will not forsake us.

The credit and reputation of the USA could be upset by prevailing financial conditions. The common people may believe that the nation's business outlook is unfavorable to them. Thus, they could criticize the government's way of handling business. The masses may insist on the administration making changes which could benefit the people; thus, helping their finances. The public's emotions could surface if nothing is done by the President to improve their financial outlook. A large number of people may blame the administration for their problems, especially when their income fluctuates and the stock market rises and falls.

Rumors then could be spread that banks, and the government, are on the verge of bankruptcy. Congress will be working long hours and disagree on how to handle all the upheavals. Americans who rebel could be jailed. Disruption occurs in Congress; some members may suddenly resign, quit or walk off the job. Unreliable people in the government could be exposed and receive bad publicity that upsets the people and the economy. The Air Force needs to be alert; civil air control and all agencies that deal with space programs, air pollution and weather predicting could have major upheavals. Some American citizens may want to overthrow the government. Things are not the same. The consumer is erratic with these new, sudden and marked changes from old conditions. The public will not take to anything that is completely different and that makes them live a topsy-turvy and unstable lifestyle. Plans made can be broken. Cancellations occur. This is an ultra-progressive time – new inventions, electronic devices can bring changes. But some of these changes are not liked by the majority of people. The credit and reputation of the US is affected and our business and influence in world affairs could be damaged but not ruined.

We may not be in the power position of the past. But Americans, even the administration and its staff, are very independent. Our credit rating could go down.

National disasters cost plenty and change the lives of many. Earthquakes could be costly to the nation and individuals. Floods, tornados and hurricanes could occur without warning from geologists or the weather bureau.

The farmer could suffer when bad weather (floods, drought, hurricanes, tornadoes) damage crops. Agricultural products could be scarce. Grain, or other stored products could be heavily damaged by the weather. Land and building owners lose lots of money because people can't pay the rent, or tenants move, or the owner can't pay bills, taxes, thus foreclosure is imminent. Due to a bad economy, many people are homeless and starving. Housing problems exist. Lives are lost in floods, hurricanes, tornadoes, and earthquakes. Real estate buys could be a bargain for those who have cash to pay for them.

The Federal Reserve could buy huge amounts of Bonds which they think will improve the economy. People rebel against it. If they do take action along these lines, our monetary problems will be worse. Banks could close overnight.

People could break the rules and do not want discipline and system. Unconventional methods are the norm; those in authorities – they want the old establishment (regime) out. They revolt over how the USA is being handled by those in power. Many Americans during this time are unsynchronized, mixed up, mentally distracted, thoughtless, and unsettled. They oppose and are adverse to those in high political positions. Things in the government seem to topple. Homes could be abandoned. Terminations are the order of the day; mainly with the government, banks, and rebellious Americans. The administration needs to be heavily guarded as to their living quarters and places where they perform their jobs. The political party that is out of power can oppose the ruling party, especially when Congress meets or in doing an exposé on a member of the current regime. The President could have one shock after another and bad press. But, in spite of this, there are favorable aspects in at the same time that could save Americans financially.

****

November 22, 2013 - November 21, 2014 and December 15, 2015 - December 4. 2016

The USA's business outlook and its influence in world affairs have many problems and obstacles to overcome. The wealth and personal property of the people and their source of income is affected during this time. The banks, National Treasury, and non-speculative bonds and securities bear difficulties for the people which could get unfavorable publicity, especially when the administration is involved.

There is a lot of press about the administration and its efforts to improve the finances of the people. Gold, the banks, the nation treasury, and non-speculative bonds and securities remain in the news. The public should not rush enthusiastically into gold investing; the best approach is to be conservative. Capitalism is in the news, especially with those in the ruling class and wealthy owners of business.

The public feels uneasy in an unsteady economy, thus they are hesitant when it comes to spending, or investing money. Some people may want to withdraw their money from the banks, because they are afraid the banks will topple. Pandemonium occurs, if the general public reacts hastily, emotionally and without thinking things thoroughly through. The citizens of the USA tend to have clogged minds with making the right decision.

****

There will always be ups and downs with the money of the general public, due to the Moon which causes fluctuations. Therefore, all of the following aspects highlight the areas of life that involve the Moon.

****

March 7 – April 19, 2013 and November 30, 2015 – January 2, 2016

The public is in a good frame of mind and will spend money on personal possessions, food and retail items.

****

March 17 – April 17, 2013, September 6, 2014 – October 7, 2014
December 12, 2016 – January 1, 2017

The people are angry and emotionally frustrated over finances. There are too many ups and downs with their earnings, spending, the banks, and the National Treasury. Also tension and strife over the money spent on the armed forces, and on-going revelations of prison and nursing home abuse. Food prices are up.

However, at the same time and up to September 21, 2016 (and reinforce with extra energy June 1 – July 3, 2013 and September 19 – October 19, 2015) --- there are moments when the economy seems to be improved, thus people go on spending sprees. There is a struggle to get what they want, and in so doing, they are victorious. The retail trade should be very good.

****

February 8 – May 3, 2013 and June 9 – September 2, 2013

The public needs to be careful with looking through rose-colored glasses and thus, go on a foolish splurge. People may expect too much in money matters. But July 16 – August 16 and November 10 – December 11, 2013, there is a slight boost with the retail shops and people spending cash on entertainment, especially movies. Congress could give some aid to the oil and aviation industry (enormous sums needed to help them and the economy). Oil and aviation prices could surge from October 21 – November 21, 2014 and February 14 – March 17, 2015 --- fuel can skyrocket in price causing irritations by the consumer who drives a car or flies in an airplane. Smog could be troublesome in major cities. Pollution is at an all time high.

****

May 30 – June 29, 2013; March 26 – April 26, 2016

The economy gets a boost from tolls on expressways, public transportation, communication devices, newspapers, books, magazines, the internet, office equipment, construction equipment and neighboring countries. Also enhanced is farming, fishing, agriculture, water resources, food and dairy resources. Retail business is up. The public makes good decisions about how they should spend their money.

****

April 15 – July 9, 2013; June 13- July 13, 2014; November 9, 2014 – February 9, 2015; June 5, 2015 – July 5, 2015; September 3 – October 4, 2016; December 12, 2016 – January 11, 2017

There is a slight decline in the dollar and economy upsets, and delays, with employment checks, social security payments, taxes, insurance, welfare, taxes, lend lease between countries, the minimum wage, pensions, and a slight downtrend in the economic cycle, the National Debt and retirement benefits.

Money losses through the stock market and other forms of investment. Lots of concern over finances, debts of the nation and the inability of other countries to pay the USA moneys owed. Foreign commerce, business and the American market could slow down. There is concern over banks, transportation and the National Treasury. This is the time when the public could worry about income, possessions and money.

The US Postal Service may lose lots of revenue. Domestic and international mail gets slowed down due to transportation problems. The Americans want the price of postage reduced; the media gives this a lot space in the newspapers.

The President and his staff could receive bad press about the economy and what is being done, or not done on behalf of the American people. Groceries, commodities, farming, agriculture, fishing, water resources, dairy products and the retail trade are also in the news at this time. However, there is an improvement in these areas. Many people will hoard food and store it in their pantries. Many think food will be scarce; many believe a famine is in. Restaurants could suffer; however, fast food places fare well with inexpensive prices. Be ready for lower prices on goods, food and services. Bargains and discounts can be easily found, especially when a store is going out of business. People spend their money for the basic necessities; it is not the time to spend for luxuries – but the rich will spend money on expensive items and not think twice about it.

However, there are favorable aspects in at the same time, thereby, making it a time of doubt one moment, and confidence that the economy will turn around the next moment. There is a slight upswing, thus there is some more stability felt with the plans made by the administration and a small improvement in the economy and employment areas.

Negotiations involving foreign aid are a slight boost to the national economy. Measures to help the farmers and miners can be studied thoroughly.

****

July 5 – August 4 and August 31 – October 1, 2013

People, especially the radicals, rebel at prices and the economy in general. A variety of upheavals with the administration and President Obama could bring these radicals out in droves. Suddenly, money and the economy cause shocks, changes; however, there are some changes that will ultimately benefit everyone concerned. New products and inventions could flourish and be in the news. Then, later, a recall on new products, cars or computer or electronic devices could cause upsets with the consumer as well as the retail shops.

****

July 22 – August 25, 2013

Cosmetic, beauty items, and fashion prices could soar. Women will spend plenty on jewelry and parties. Art galleries may not do as well with buyers and attendance. It seems that all the luxury items have increased enormously. This could hurt the retail trade, when the purchases are by the average person. But the wealthy class won't blink over how much they pay.

****

July 22 – August 21, 2013; July 25 – August 27, 2014; September 15 – October 16, 2015

The consumer is restless concerning finances; ups and downs with mood switches; Irritations, obstacles and aggravations with money matters. Their emotions are on how they can handle family members regarding their income. The problems they think they have are not as bad as they feel.

****

August 9 – September 12, 2013; July 3 – August 2, 2016

Clashes between the government and the common classes over money issues – their pride gets hurt when they can't give their families the care that is needed. They may blame it on the government. The President and the administration are aggravated while they look for a better way to appease the public.

****

September 18 – October 19, 2013; November 15 – December 16, 2015

The press reports the confusion the public and administration have over the economy. There is much indecision by those in power to do anything. Misinterpretations, misquotes by the media upset the public. Misunderstandings occur. Interviews by the President may create obstacles with how the populace responds to him about financial issues.

****

January 14 – February 14, 2014; March 7 – April 6, 2014

One group may not be cooperative with another group. They refuse to meet, however, if they do get together, they try to use force on each other. Divided opinions and views between these groups and the general public. Protests and crusades could be costly, especially in protecting the people by hiring more policemen. Smugglers, spies, terrorists, bombs and nuclear waste could be on TV and radio continuously. Airports need protection and those that work there need to be investigated. The Supreme Court could be called in to make decisions which cause drastic changes to the general populace. The public outcry can be heard worldwide. Obstacles with money and the economy get bad press. The public may rebel against President Obama and his action along these lines. They believe the government is forcing these issues.

****

May 18 – June 18, 2014; December 14, 2014 – March 30, 2015

The public spends lots of money on cosmetics, perfume, beauty treatments, clothes, jewelry and all luxury goods. Parties are in the news, especially with those who are rich and in society. Social events involving peace treaties could go rather smoothly. The Department of Treasury could report good news about the people's money. The economy seems to be growing. The retail trade could pick up considerably.

****

September 1 – October 3, 2014; June 22 – July 23, 2015

Good luck with sales. The retailers are as happy as the people who spend money on their merchandise. Expansion in business is seen. Everyone is optimistic. Higher prices are in but the public doesn't care, especially with those who are wealthy. Capitalism is at an all-time high. International trade grows. Treaties are favored by everyone involved. It seems to be a prosperous time. Congress, Goodwill Missions and Ambassadors are in the news. The public feels philanthropic. Happiness seems to prevail.

****

October 21 – November 21, 2014; February 14 – March 17, 2015

People need to watch out for con artists, swindles, scams and get-rich-schemes. Foolish money splurges are in the news and can bring disappointments. Gas, Oil, and Petroleum could be too costly. Promises made by these companies or the administration could fall through. Deceptive methods are employed. Inflation is high. The public is blind to financial deals. They need to be alert and be realistic instead of emotionally being in Shangri-la. Movies cost more as well as all forms of entertainment. Drug addiction is worse. There could be scandals involving pharmaceutical companies. Food can be poisoned and on recall. Aviation prices are up.

****

December 27, 2014 – January 29, 2015; April 2 – May 3, 2015

Good luck prevails with President Obama, his staff and the general populace. Money appears to be good, especially gold. Those officials in the government are working in behalf of the public. The press reports events that are favorable to the administration and that are beneficial to the common classes of people.

Money spent on the White House and the dignitaries they entertain is in the news. There are improvements relative to housing, crops on the ground – farming, and mining. More hotels and buildings are built, because those involved see the economy improving. Business owners are pleased with the government and, as a result, of the money they are making.

****

May 10 – June 9, 2015; June 19 – July 22, 2016

The press gives the President and the economy bad publicity. The public is irritated because it affects their finances. The populace does not approve everything employed by the administration. Because of the media, the retail trade is down.

****

December 15, 2012 – January 14, 2013; December 5, 2015 – January 5, 2016;
September 20 – October 20, 2016

The public is overly confident that their money and business is increasing. The growth factor for income and sales picks up; however, the President and the general populace are too carried away with optimism. Therefore, spending by Congress, President Obama and the common people can be at an all-time high. Inflation could affect everyone. Capitalism and philanthropy is expanding. Some people in business could over expand and charge higher prices.

****

July 21 – August 20, 2016; September 11 – October 11, 2016

It is a favorable time for companies and corporations, to reach the masses through chain stores, restaurant and fast-food chain franchises. People spend money on international and interstate commerce (importing, exporting) and travel. Pacts of treaties can be signed, in the news and the public is in favor of these transactions. Spies and terrorists could be captured.

Money is spent on radios, television sets, digital music, and recordings and on web sites, wireless devices and transmission; CDs and disks. They make a lot of money for the corporations who own them.

It seems to be that everyone is cooperative with each other. A spiritual time for the masses could receive good publicity. Various religious groups are pleasant to each other. Nuclear treaties with overseas countries make people feel safe. The FBI, CIA, police, and covert operatives who work undercover can be in the news for all of the benefits they bring to the world. People are not as worried about their jobs or money as they have been at other times.

EMPLOYMENT

In to January 13, 2013; October 24, 2013 – September 18, 2014

Many people will get laid off or fired. Some businesses will fold. Terminations of employment, because of new technology and the workers do not know how to operate the computer or electronic devices or it could be the company is moving to a new location. Also, new methods are employed in a company that eliminates the need for many employees. It is an erratic time for money and those who work in a job that gives service to others, as well as office labor. Shocks with many upheavals such as strikes. The Food and Drug Administration could close down a business. Anything can happen – it is unpredictable. The radical element could cause problems with the economy which could affect a business, thus, getting rid of troublemakers. Problems could involve the Air Force, NASA, Civil Air Control and all agencies that deal with space programs, Air Pollution and the Weather. Legislatures and Congressional representatives could resign or suddenly quit or get fired. People that are radical feel like breaking the rules and can be involved with an exposé. These people are disgusted with the old manner in which everything gets done, thus they bring chaos, upsets and try to bring change. Controversy gets a lot of publicity. President Obama attracts upheavals with a change in his cabinet or, perhaps, he is in shock with those who work directly under him. Thus, disagreements are cancelled and so are parties. Sudden events transpire that cause him to be on call 24/7.

****

In to November 16, 2015

There is employment for those in the arts, television, radio, web-design, internet, catering to the masses, fashion, jewelry, beauty; especially with companies that have chain stores, large corporations, candy that is mass produced, and those who work for unions, federations, foundations, franchised boutiques, and fast food chains.

****

In Now and for the Upcoming Years

Those who work in sales can do very well, especially art, art objects, wigs, cosmetics, jewelry, clothes, music, beauty areas and party accessories; wedding planners and those who deal with party business, such as sending invitations, baking pastry and catering.

****

In to October 2, 2018

Those employed in the arts, music and the current regime can hold their jobs and gain respect, admiration and favorable publicity. It helps if they give, or go to, office or political parties. Socializing as part of their profession keeps them employed and in the limelight. However, there is criticism from the press because of the lavish spending done by the administration. However, this does not interfere with their employment.

Crops, grains and farming areas due to bad weather may create a loss of work, especially to land laborers. Basic utility jobs and mining areas could be slow hiring.

****

In to October 22, 2033

Many of the laborers in the arts, entertainment, amusement, fashion, beauty catering, restaurant, the stock market and legislature have steady jobs. Employment in some of these areas steadily rise; also, those who work in banks and handle the money of others. These jobs, if they involve socializing, so much the better, also, if being courteous is part of the occupation. Many, who have been employed for a long time, or elderly workers, can benefit. Those who work in health care, hospitals, rehab centers and take care of those who are ill – these jobs are needed and keep people employed regardless of the economy. (If someone's horoscope is discordant, it is possible they could be unemployed.) Those who work in the tax and unemployment office or human resources can do well. People who have jobs in amusement centers, theme parks, schools, the stock exchange and banks, make money and don't have to worry that much about their employment.

****

In to September 21, 2016

Good luck for those who work in the following fields: mechanics, engineering, health care, food (brokers, distributors, restaurants, bars, groceries, catering), public service, civil service, prisons, jails, hospitals, manufacturing, liquor (stores, bartenders), dentists, doctors, dental hygienists, athletes, the military and Department of Defense.

Those who work in dangerous areas, such as construction, fire and police work, athletics (boxing), explosives, guns, ammunition, knives, scissors, the military and mechanical – can easily attract accidents, injuries, violence and strife from January 25, 2015 to April 26, 2016. These dates are the worst, however, danger areas of employment always is a risk and can attract hazards.

****

In to February 5, 2017

There are jobs in aviation (especially for mechanics), designing theme parks and logos for movies, sporting events, pharmacology and pharmaceuticals, petroleum, oil, pipe lines, construction, manufacturing (the designing part), gas station and Oil industry that involves cosmetics (soap, candles, perfume, cosmetics, etc). There can be hazards in these fields such as in the Oil industry – the oil spills.

****

In to February 9, 2026

There are delays with getting a job. The employment rate decreases, only to turn around and be good for some people. However, there are job cuts, salary reductions, outsourcing – thus, workers are concerned about their money and many find themselves in dire conditions – like losing their homes because they can't pay the rent or mortgage. Cheap foreign labor overseas or those who enter our country will work at almost anything, thus, taking jobs from Americans who live in the USA. These USA citizens refuse to labor with low wages. Due to these issues, there is a slowdown in the American market of goods imported overseas and many find themselves poverty stricken, on unemployment and suffering hunger, especially when they can't feed their loved ones. There are some manufacturing, or agencies, that will cut corners such as advertising and publishing fields. Teachers, space and communication fields could downsize, thus many are jobless.

****

In Now and for the Upcoming Years

The unemployment rate gets bad press; although, there will be times when publicity is inclined to favor people getting hired for jobs. Many owners of business will either close down, or have a reduction of employees and salary cuts. They are trying to be conservative. The minimum wage is a problem in some areas, because there are business owners who don't even want to pay that. Then there are some employers who pay some of their employees good wages, but others are not treated the same. These types of businesses fluctuate between being great to doing poorly. Uncertainty for employees continues to escalate. Many people, who have lost their jobs, are becoming self employed. Therefore, go after employment by taking immediate action – but be patient if things don't happen overnight. If you aren't mobile, assertive and aggressive it will be difficult to get work – you need to be an eager beaver.

There are many disappointments with jobs in the oil, motion pictures, Merchant Marine, oceanography, public relations, stock companies, hospitals, prisons, aviation, petroleum, gas stations, and prescription drug business. Generic drugs are less expensive and more Americans are buying them; thus, the pharmaceutical companies attract a loss of revenue and cut down on the employees they hire.

Farms, crops, mines, coal, glue, asphalt and the necessity areas can have losses and not hire as many people as they did in the past. The USA's business and influence in world affairs suffers due to a bad economy and a lessening of people to do the work. However, there are favorable dates as mentioned previously – it is best to try to get work in the areas that are hiring, which means many Americans need to learn a new trade. When work is slow to come by – make a change. Do not stay home and get depressed or live in the past. Take action and maybe you will get lucky and get hired in a new field.

****

In Now and for the Upcoming Years

There are many assembly-line jobs, mass production (with manufactures), labor unions, foundations, agencies that deal with waste control and abortion; police, detective and investigative work; research; FBI, CIA, DEA, IRS, bodyguards, spy work, Special Forces Operative who with the FBI, CIA, police, Interpol, and other agencies around the globe. Teamwork with these various groups cooperating and exchanging information is beneficial for the good of the universe. The President could delegate a group of people (a committee) and give them the responsibility of deciding what is good for the American people, and how best to obtain favorable results. Those chosen to be part of a team effort will be paid and will attempt to carry out the administration's plans. The Supreme Court can be involved too. Convention work can employ lots of people; little by little an increase of jobs along those lines will be seen. There are lucrative jobs in high positions with large corporations, especially when these companies merge. The occupation favored is International Trade and Commerce. Agencies that handle higher education and immigration are good jobs to have, as well as some bank occupations and work in non-speculative bonds and securities.

Corporate jobs could open up; also, those companies who employ mass production; spies, placement, detectives; waste control agencies, abortion clinics; retreats, fast food and other chain restaurants; the Department of Agriculture, public transportation, roads; water and dairy resources, farming; retail stores; chemicals; researchers, and surveyors.

Other fields that are beneficial for employment: Radio, television, cable, recording industry, internet, Research, Medical, Investigative, Nuclear, microchip, wireless gadgets and transmissions, Web sites, disks, bodyguards, covert operatives, foreign shipping, satellites, and corporations. However, a the same time there are those fields which could employ a person – there are many who are unemployed either because they don't have the ability or education needed or their own individual horoscope is afflicted. Taking a course in these areas can improve a person's chances of getting back into the work force.

****

In to September 21, 2016 but reinforced with additional energy September 6 – October 7, 2014; September 19 – October 19, 2015; December 12, 2016 – January 1, 2017

Impatience with looking for a job, however, by pushing and taking the initiative, it helps getting hired. Without action nothing can happen. Remember, "Rome was not built in a day." There are many jobs available in a business where an individual serves others, such as the health care, restaurant, food industry, military and manufacturing as a sales person.

****

November 10, 2013 – December 11, 2013; January 23 – February 23, 2016; May 16 – June 15, 2016

Jobs could be available in the motion picture industry, aviation, Oil field, plastics, swimming pool, Oceanography, Merchant Marine, marine Scientist, stock market, public relations, pharmaceutical, Gas station, soaps, candles and photography.

****

March 26 – April 26, 2016

Jobs could be available in the literary field, information, journalist, reporter, postal service, courier business, roads, transportation, communication, highways, education and printing. Also Agents, dispatchers, taxi, garage, parking lots.

****

June 13 – July 13, 2014; November 9, 2014 – February 9, 2015; June 5 – July 5, 2015; September 3 – October 4, 2016; December 12, 2016 – January 11, 2017

Delays and problems to find work. The economy isn't as good and one has to take on added work – even a menial job. The unemployment line could be long. Ambition and persistence is needed. The jobs available could be low wages: Storage work, grains, farms, harvesting, lands and work in coal, or other mines. Service jobs, housekeeping, cleaning (clothes or janitor) and management could be available.

****

September 12 – October 1, 2013

Jobs that don't last long, such as part time work could be easier to get. Modern, new products or technology labor is up and down. It is an unpredictable job market. Expect the unexpected, especially with government or civil service work.

****

July 25 – August 27, 2014; September 15 – October 16, 2015

The public is restless and jobs fluctuate, especially those dealing with food, feminine areas and retail. Fishing, agriculture, dairy and water resource jobs are possible. Daily changes in employment.

****

September 18 – October 19, 2013; November 15 – December 16, 2015

Writing, mental work, telephone, communications, transportation, postal or courier work, printing, railroads, newspaper, periodicals and magazine work is difficult to get. Office work or equipment could get bad press, thus, work in these areas isn't the "in" thing. Education could be at a standstill. Travel could be "iffy." Too much confusion with conflicting reports by employment agencies and the news media. Misquotes and misinterpretations with jobs offered in the newspapers or on the internet. Mistakes in print could be the problem.

****

January 14 – February 14, 2014; March 7 – April 6, 2014

Obstacles with work in the recruiting field, television, radio, cable, satellite, court, publishing advertising, foreign shipping, international travel, nuclear, waste control, microchip, wireless transmission, web sites, recording industry, franchised fast-food or department or boutique fields. Police work, CIA, FBI, Security agencies and surveillance systems, and foundations – they all could be difficult to get. Investigations could cause problems for many.

****

May 18 – June 18, 2014; December 14, 2014 – March 30, 2015

Jobs in banks and where financial transactions take place could be open to the populace now. It may be easier to get hired, also, in beauty fields (cosmetics make up, hairdresser, facials, and spas), fashion, textile industry, perfume, jewelry, artistic areas, music, party business, weddings, receptionist and manicure field. Social events can be in the news, especially with President Obama playing host to VIPs. Our influence in world affairs is good. It is a favorable time for the reputation and credit of the USA.

****

September 1, 2014 – October 3, 2014; June 22, 2015 – July 23, 2015

Good luck for the banking industry and financial transactions and working in these areas as well as those who work in non-speculative bonds and securities, the treasury department, religion, international trade, commerce, merchandising, marketing, selling, agencies who work in immigration, higher education, ambassadors, congress and legislative fields. All of the preceding is in the news and is good for the image of the USA, President and his staff. These jobs could have an increase in pay now.

****

October 21 – November 21, 2014; February 14- March 17, 2015

Jobs in the aviation, film industry, merchant marine, oceanography, gas, oil, petroleum, candles, plastics, soaps, photography, stock market brokers or anyone who works in any of these fields – problems, irritations, criticism occur. Con artists, scams, swindles could be in the news and give a bad name to the USA and people could blame President Obama and promises made by him and those in congress, legislature, his staff, administration for the fall out or existing difficulties in these areas. It is not a favorable time for jobs in any of these fields.

****

December 27, 2014 – January 29, 2015; April 2 – May 3, 2015

Good luck in the political field, executive job market, administrative fields – it is easier to get hired now in these areas. Also in banking, bonds, the treasury (jobs as a treasurer as well as working as a cashier – handling money), real estate, land occupations, agricultural and weather careers; also employment in shipping centers (building or working), malls, plazas, hotels and a good time (if your horoscope is also good) to go into business for oneself. The President is in the news in a beneficial way, money of the people increases, promotions and raises in salary or good paying jobs are out there, the credit of the USA and its reputation in world affairs is at an all time high.

****

December 5, 2015 – January 5, 2016; September 20 – October 20, 2016

People are overly confident that jobs in sales, commissions, and bonuses will be high. But everything is not as hoped, even though increases are in. Jobs in banking, publishing, advertising, international trade and commerce, financial institutions, immigration, marketing and congress could be overly exaggerated at this time and everyone has high hopes that a fortune will be made in these areas.

****

May 10 – June 9, 2015; June 19 – July 22, 2016

The employment rate receives bad publicity and President Obama is criticized by the press for being the cause of it. Those who work in banking, transportation and the communication fields also get unfavorable publicity.

****

July 3 – August 2, 2016

Aggravations with the people and employment. The President and administration get blamed, and receive bad publicity for the job market. The vitality of the average person is down when it comes to looking for a job. They believe that the government and owners of business are not helping them when it comes to work. Thus, their income is at stake and officials seem to ignore them. This could be with housing, farming, mining, logging, their lands, property, buildings, hotels, renting houses or tents they live in because of damage to their by homes by tornadoes, floods, earthquakes and hurricanes. They can also be upset with FEMA, the mayor or governor.

****

July 21 – August 20, 2016; September 11 – October 11, 2016

Opportunities in employment for those in police work, firemen, civil servants, television, cable, radio, recording industry, United Nations, Nuclear energy, microchip, wireless devices, CDs, disks, the FBI, CIA, covert operatives, IRS, security and surveillance agencies, homeland security, TSA, agencies that deal with waste control and abortion, research, medical, health care, restaurants, cafeterias, diners, places where food and drink are dispensed, Food and Drug Administration, armed forces, foreign shipping, interstate and international commerce and traffic treaties, travel agencies, space programs, satellites, interstate airplane traffic, the law and courts, publishing and advertising.

Teamwork and cooperation is favorable. Companies, corporations, franchises, chain stores and all group participation jobs are favorable. The news is favorable for the USA and President Obama. Our world leadership is acknowledged by those in various countries around the globe. United Nations and NATO are also involved, thus bring employment and recognition to everyone involved.

THE STOCK MARKET

In until March 16, 2013

Investors will be aggressive, risk-taking and speculation could pay off some of the time. Due to some discordant aspects, this can fluctuate. However some speculative stocks based upon military production, surgical instruments, steel, scissors, manufactured items, liquor, sports equipment and machinery used in construction and destruction could go up fast. Many Americans will jump in and sell quickly. A quick profit can be made; others are confident that it'll go higher, so they hang on to their stock in these areas.

Many of these stocks will change daily (it depends upon your horoscope and how the stock market division is – harmonious or inharmonious.), but can bring good luck even though September 21, 2016 could be lucky for risk-takers. However, already in for years and escalating to February 4, 2026, there is a time when it is not good for taking chances. Investors have to be careful in all of these investment areas; many will clean up, others will lose (it depends upon a person's individual horoscope as how they will fare in anything invested in the stock market). There can be a loss of money by manufacturing concerns; stocks in these companies may gradually get low, but could rise up again. Many Americans could lose, although if they hold on long enough, many of these stocks could regain a favorable position.

****

January 24, 2015 – April 26, 2016

A very risky time. Investors will be torn whether they should leap in or stay out of the market. Stocks involving military equipment, guns, ammunition, tools, knives and machinery could make people leap in, especially if we are war with foreign nations. But there are others who will hold back from speculative investing (that is until February 4, 2016). Either they will wait too long to invest or jump in too fast. They battle between being impulsive or using extreme caution. There will always be those individuals who would rather take a risk than to let something pass by.

****

In until February 4, 2013

There is some fortunate news that boosts the stock market. Unexpected discoveries, inventions, new concepts, and technology, computers, gadgets and items for the Air Force, NASA, Civil Air Control and all agencies that deal with the space programs, air pollution and weather predicting that benefit the stock market. Legislators, congressional representatives and the President are favored and the USA's reputation, credit, business and influence in world affairs are a great aid to the stock market.

****

May 3, 2014 – March 29, 2015

Investors can be indecisive and confused about taking a chance with art objects, cosmetics, perfume, jewelry, textiles, fashion, music, and any area connected with beauty items. Money could easily be lost in these areas during this time due to the timing of when to, or not to, invest. Obstacles with communication are a problem as well as the press giving bad coverage to these industrial concerns. Perhaps, an investor reads something in a newspaper, magazine or hears reporters talking adversely or writing confusing facts. Also involved are telephones (land phones) and objects used for transportation. Stocks during this time could affect modern, new items or companies.

However, in for the years to come and escalating until October 22, 2033, the following stocks can do well – but it is iffy during the May 2014 to March 2015 dates: Cosmetics, beauty items, wigs, textiles, fashion, perfume, jewelry, art, ceramics, statues, pottery, curios, gloves, puppets, dolls, confectionery, purses, hats, shoes, millinery, beads, sequins, furs, flowers, music and party accessories.

Those who are interested in stock seriously will study and scrutinize everything before they spend money on a portfolio. They tend to be patient, ultra-conservative and use common sense. They are good at trading and using strategy. Those who wait too long to invest and are fearful, should refrain from investing. The stock market and the economy will be up and down at this time. Some who invest in art, fashion and beauty areas as well as jewelry will fare well by being conservative and holding on to these stocks for a long time. Note: Stocks with established companies do best during this date. In other words, a business that has been a brand name for a long time and has made money steadily over the years.

****

In and escalating to August 13, 2013

Speculative stocks in the communication and transportation industry, magazine and newspaper areas may be reported by the media to be good for investment purposes. However, think twice before going out on a limb. Inflation and overprices abound. The public could pay a high price for stock in these areas and later regret it. Selling stock at this time doesn't pay. Profits are not as great as many will take a risk. Don't believe all that you read.

****

November 22, 2013 – November 21, 2014

Due to bad news in the political field, the stock market could be affected. People are confused and indecisive, especially about those in power. Money can be unwisely invested, in property, buildings, hotels, shopping centers, agricultural products, mining. Disasters such as hurricanes, tornados, earthquakes and typhoons could be involved.

Due to idle rumors and bad news as reported by the media, the stock market is likely to be unsteady. Pandemonium reigns when people are confused and perplexed as to how they should invest money; others are concerned about their jobs – will they have a paycut or be one of the many who are unemployed? Should they spend their money on stock, fun or take it out of the bank and hide it?

****

June 18, 2014 – May 31, 2015

However, within these dates, a favorable time is indicated in the areas of communication, travel and educational materials, such as books or teaching devices. Many investors will make their decisions based on facts reported by the press – newspapers, magazines, talk shows. Transportation, office equipment, construction equipment such as steamrollers, skip hoes, and the like. The Internet brings many opportunities that can benefit those who study the market and make wise choices with their money. Neighboring countries such as Canada or Mexico can attract investors who may want to invest in the stock of a company.

****

In Now and for the Upcoming Years

Also, during this time, the stock market will have heavy losses and then heavy gains. One moment capitalism with high prices and gains. Conservativeness and low prices are in – with some people attracting a loss. The public fluctuates between being confident the market will soar and having a lack of confidence it will crash. There is stability one moment and the next moment the market is unstable. Many people will sell before the stock is too low and invest in art or gold. There will be many investors who will have enormous gains, while others lose their shirt. Some people are not afraid of taking a risk, while others will fear the market is close to crashing and sell stock at a loss. Many want to reap the harvest on a large scale, whereas, others are satisfied to make small profits. The unemployment factor is a contributing agent to losses. The public becomes nervous, unsure and is fearful they will be on poverty row. Many will experience losses and others will try to protect themselves against losses.

****

In Now and for the Upcoming Years

Stocks in the motion picture industry, aviation, oil, theme parks and gambling (casinos) could be iffy and cause losses. Gas prices can rise; inflation is in. The aviation industry gradually loses money; people are afraid to fly due to a fear of a crash, or they want added security, which could cause many airlines to go bankrupt. Congress may promise to bail them out, but unfortunately, it is not enough to save many airlines. This can put a drain on America's monetary supply, which upsets the stock market. The watering of stocks (inflation) and promotional schemes could cause many cases of fraud – many are jailed for fraudulent schemes, hedge funds or inside trading. Americans could throw caution to the winds in the hope of some wonderful gain. Caution and conservativeness need to be exercised.

Theme parks could have their attendance down; this affects those stocks. Also, those who take wild risks could lose out. Greed, lies and deception abound when people fall for promises of huge gains, like those who lost everything with being cheated in the hedge-fund area.

The worst time for these occurrences is from November 22, 2016 – February 19, 2018. There is some mixed press in these areas up to September 15, 2014. Also, there are some rather good investments in oil, gas, petroleum, aviation, soaps, candles, plastics, oceanography and marine science investments. The film and motion picture industry and theme parks – all part of entertainment --- in until May 19, 2013 and November 10, 2015 – September 28, 2016. Theme parks and art could also be favorable.

****

The progressed Moon in the USA's horoscope is traveling thru the stock market house, thus causing fluctuations – more than usual – during the following dates when it is very volatile with many ups and downs.

****

December 15, 2012 – January 14, 2013

Expectations high, over confidence reigns, selling is not receiving the big gains hoped for. Merchandising gains makes people get carried away.

****

February 8 – May 3, 2013; June 9 – September 2, 2013

Pharmaceuticals, film, the motion picture industry, theme parks, gas, oil, petroleum, aviation, plastics, items used for swimming pools, resort areas, candles and soaps are speculative and could bring some gain or disappointments when they turn out to be a bad investment. The picture painted could be rosy and some companies may make good earnings but others will not be as expected. Caution is needed with anything that sounds too good to be true.

****

March 7 – April 7, 2013

Groceries, commodities and items needed for the home, vending machines, water resources, agriculture, dairy, and fishing areas could be up during this time.

****

March 17 – April 17, 2013; June 23 – September 15, 2013

Impatience, risk-taking and impulsive buying, selling and trading should be avoided. However, some stocks could do well, such as manufacturing companies, liquor, guns, knives, sharp instruments (surgical equipment), steel, scissors, sports equipment, machinery used in construction or destruction and farming equipment.

****

March 18 – April 19, 2013

Investors are in a good frame of mind and can profit, especially in areas involving foreign nations, silver, groceries, commodities, home products, feminine items, fishing, water, dairy and farming.

****

April 15 – July 9, 2013

Money losses can occur through the stock market and other forms of investment. Lots of concern over the economy, national debts and the inability (or delays) of other nations to pay the USA monies owed. Foreign commerce, business and the American market could slow down. A concern over banks, the National Treasury and transportation is part of the problem. Lands, crops, farming, mining, the unemployment, basic utilities, agriculture, hay, grain, wheat, timber, lumber, soybeans, coal, commodities, rye barley, oats, ores, minerals, preservatives, antiques, coins, blue chip stocks, and necessities – can be down at this time. However, there will be those who will buy at the lower price and later benefit.

****

May 30 – June 29, 2013

Opportunity to do well with stocks, especially periodicals, magazines, newspapers, public transportation, highways and roads. By reading and studying everything relative to these areas will be of great help to the investors. Some food, commodities, farming, fishing, water and dairy areas tend to be favorable, as well as transportation, paper, communications, books and informational devices.

****

June 1 – July 2, 2013

Investors who take quick action can end up being a winner. However, the areas that are highlighted during this time are stocks involving food, dairy, fishing , agriculture, water resources, sewing tools, cooking equipment, feminine items, vending machines, retail stores, knives, guns, ammunition, machinery, equipment for building – construction-destruction, surgical instruments, military equipment, music, liquor and firecrackers.

****

July 5 – August 4, 2013; August 31 – September 12, 2013

Stocks could go wild and crazy, topsy-turvy, up and down, unpredictable. Many investors could be too erratic and take sudden action that could result in upsets. Others may be penetrative, progressive and scientifically go after the stock they intuitively believe in. Inventions, new technology, computers, gadgets, fads, the latest "in" product, any item that is unique, different, outer-space areas, and anything that is ultra-progressive is highlighted at this time. It is a very unpredictable time involving these types of stocks. Controversy prevails and the radical element brings mixed decisions.

****

July 16 – August 16, 2013

Investors are in the mood to get rich overnight and could get too carried away looking through rose-colored glasses. Exaggerations by promoters make people think they will earn big returns on their money. However, many will have gains in pharmaceuticals, oceanography, marine science, movies, film, oil, gas, petroleum, plastics, candles, soaps, theme parks, aviation and resorts. Some casinos, places of amusement, stadiums, arenas, food, fishing, agriculture, boats, swimming pools and water resources could be slightly beneficial during these dates. An investigation of the facts, analytical thinking and practicality need to be employed.

****

July 22 – August 21, 2013

Aggravations with lots of confusion for investors. An unfavorable time, with indecision by the common people and stocks which involve food, commodities, fish, water resources, agriculture, feminine items, dairy products, sewing and cooking equipment, vending machines and retail stores. Bad publicity doesn't help matters.

****

July 22 – August 25, 2013

This is not a favorable time to invest in stocks in the areas of textiles, cosmetics, fashion, perfume, art objects, ceramics, pottery, curios, puppets, dolls, candy, cookies, sugar and carbohydrate products, jewelry, purses, millinery, gloves, beads, sequins, furs, wigs, flowers, music and party accessories. Keep in mind that if your individual horoscope is lucky along these lines, you may only be slightly affected or not at all.

****

August 9 – September 12, 2013

Aggravating news and bad publicity involving the President and administration could cause upsets to stocks, especially those involved in housing, food, agriculture, dairy products, fish, water resources, commodities products that use gold, land, the homes of the people, buildings, hotels, rooming houses, shopping centers/malls, plazas, complexes, mining, logging, and real estate. The problem could be due to hurricanes, tornados, earthquakes or typhoons.

REAL ESTATE, PROPERTY, HOUSING

In Now and for the Upcoming Years, Escalates to January 19, 2013

The housing, foreclosures and problems with farms (crops being destroyed by the weather), basic utilities on the rise and yet many are without them – as well as a slowing down of the economy with many people in debt. After January 19, 2013 this will lift. However, there are many issues causing problems in these areas, but somehow there is a saving grace with those who work hard, make sacrifices and cut down on expenses. Even though this is difficult for many, there are others who will profit in areas of land, basic utilities through October 22, 2033. Those people will be on a budget, find ways to look for bargains and take on extra added work and responsibility. Therefore, it is wise to follow a plan and curb expenses. Also, the food supply can be at a low ebb. Congress may be too slow on acting on behalf of the farmer with relief funds; thus, farmers could lose their land, homes or be heavily in debt. Delays are in to protect the public's health through disease control.

****

April 24. 2013 – April 23, 2014

There can be many shocks and upheavals between the working class and politicians. Earthquakes, floods, tornadoes and all types of disasters can occur. Homes will be destroyed, land will be upturned, crops will be ruined and the price Americans pay for goods will skyrocket. The people of the USA will rebel.

Homes are damaged by storms and floods; many homeowners are uninsured against these disasters. Those who are insured could have a long wait to collect the insurance claim money due them. Also, insurance companies will have financial difficulties during these dates. Those who have insurance may not have enough coverage to bail them out. Congress may promise to come to their aid and allot disaster money. This puts another drain on the money supply of the USA and people will protest loud and clearly. Thus, the President will not like the publicity that results.

The farmer could also suffer from a drought. Agricultural products could be scarce. Grain, or other stored products could be heavily damaged by the weather. Land and building owners lose money because people can't pay their rent, or tenants move, or the owner can't pay bills, taxes, thus, foreclosure is imminent. Many people are homeless and starving and their outcry gets tons of bad publicity for those in power. Lives are lost. Housing problems prevail; money is needed for construction, but delays occur. The building business could be down; lumber is scarce and expensive. Conservationists and environmentalist cry "Don't destroy our trees!" Coal can be scarce, homes are cold. Miners could lose their jobs. The steel industry does not look good. Crude materials can be low – conservation of our natural resources and the environment could be a big issue and receive lots of bad publicity for the President.

However, with all the preceding there are those who will profit. Land and all sorts of property deals could be bargains, especially when people buy old structures and renovate them. Large corporations secure vast holdings of land at little expense when the economy is spiraling down – many people make lots of money from foreclosures that they buy at a low price. They can turn around and profit from them when they sell structures at a fair price.

During these dates the unemployed have to go without the necessities; some live in slums, others are homeless. Housing is a problem. It is a rough time for the common class of people. There is a lot of looting going on when the calamities occur. Those farmers who don't lose their crops are headed for long and hard hours of labor – nothing new for the farmer. There will be those who can profit a little from their laborious efforts. Under the ground coal, minerals and ores could boost the economy but there will be many delays in this direction from those in political positions. New concepts and revolutionary ideas will be wanted by the people; however, the change needed brings obstacles from the political arena, such as lawmakers and the President. If the President comes up with newfangled and way out ideas, the public will not go along with them.

An exposé in the government could shock the nation, especially if it involves housing, land and money. The American people during this time are abrupt, erratic, and independent and cry for change. Old conditions are not wanted; new conditions are desired. Life, as the people know, will be changed and markedly different – things will not be the same as new chapters open. Many people will want the President to step down; they will be disappointed with him and his staff. New laws will not be to the people's liking. It is a time of upheaval for the United States and people who reside here. The sudden events, shocks and upheavals will not only upset the lives of the American people but also that of the politicians.

****

November 22, 2013 – November 21, 2014

Hurricanes, tornados, earthquakes, and other national disasters that cause upsets to people's crops, homes and transportation ensue. The President could make confusing statements to the press – indecisions occur, especially with officials – FEMA and others in power. Aggravations occur because of a mix-up in communications. This is costly to the people and their money and the press has a field day with causing further confusion. Those affected are in a dither as to what to do while they wait for some kind of sign, message or word from the President and others in official positions.

****

December 5, 2015 – December 4, 2016

There are obstacles with housing, the lands, crop buildings, and the climate --- which affects those property areas as well as the stock market. The publicity is hurtful to the landowners, President and people in power. The money of the people is an issue in these areas and damages the officials, and President's reputation.

****

In Now and for the Upcoming Years and Escalating to October 2, 2018

Those who are in top positions can fare well by profiting from real estate sales. Capitalism flourishes among the wealthy and luck is on their side when it comes to land, hotels, shopping complexes, buildings and housing. There are many influential people who will make a fortune on expanding their real estate holdings. Those in the society world will throw lavish parties on their estates, especially in the name of politics for those they wish to be in power. These same classes of people will continue with their elegant parties. However, there are many people who have had money, and entertained grandly, those can no longer do so – that continues on the increase through October 2, 2018. They are overly confident and need to make an impression on those who they want to be in a power position. Gradually, they will wake up to their folly and cut corners in other areas of their life. Their egos need to show off their homes and what money can buy for them in the way of favors from VIPs in every area from the political arena to the daily business world.

The parties given by the President in the White House will be criticized due to their high cost. The so-called society element will be entertained in the style they are accustomed to. Decorating the White House could be expensive, especially by a new President after Barack Obama's term ends.

CRIME, SPIES, TERRORISTS, PLACE OF CONFINEMENT

In to February 5, 2017

The war on drugs gradually escalates as more and more Americans are addicted. Pushers get children hooked on drugs; they pose as their friends. Narcotics are prevalent in schools and colleges. Adults and children lose their lives from drug trafficking that stems from aboard. Drugs could be disguised and hidden in toys, games, sporting equipment and other products. Drugs gradually become more available in schools, colleges, amusement areas such as stadiums, arenas, and places where entertainment is dispensed.

Con artists and scams escalate; some are caught and sent to prison. Phony charitable institutions are prevalent. Murder is on the rise, even children who are doing the shooting. The promotion of violence in video games and in the motion picture industry gives youngsters ideas – they have active imaginations and thus not only children, but adults bring bodily harm to others through knife stabbings, pistol shots and other acts of violence. Accidents could occur on roller coasters or other rides that are dangerous due to mechanical failure or the mistake of a maintenance worker. Criminal activity continues to escalate. Americans are injured by each other – fights, violence, robbery and murder takes place every day.

Fireman, policemen, sheriffs and all types of law enforcement officers are killed or injured in the line of duty. Those who guard our nation, such as soldiers and members of the navy are hurt and die in combat. The country's armed forces and Special Services (Green Berets, the Rangers, Navy Seals, Delta Force) make excellent plans with maps, undercover work and use the right strategy to wipe out terrorists.

Aviation disaster – helicopters shot down and other tragedies involving our planes overseas and on American soil. Oil wells, or refineries, could be blown up by terrorists; gas and oil prices skyrocket. Thus, these areas need to be well guarded by the military.

An American cannot let up guard, even if things appear cleared up. Because these "sleeper" terrorists could suddenly, destroy Americans through explosives, accidents (that appear innocent, like with a car). Accidents, injuries and violence to the American people are likely to continue aboard.

Teams of people need to be employed when it comes to goods that arrive from overseas – even guns and ammunition could be smuggled into the USA. But the USA has a fantastic team of law-enforcement officers, customs and immigration personnel, thus, investigations can be made and the enemy's plans could be thwarted. USA secret agents, spies and the FBI and CIA work night and day, with untiring effort, to win the battle with the terrorists. The open enemy, the Taliban and others, call it a religious war. However, the Islamic religion is misrepresented by the terrorists who have been brainwashed by their leaders. Militant terrorists reside all over the world; they've been around and will continue to be around for years. They've set off bombs in Paris, London, Madrid, Israel and numerous other countries. Many of these terrorists are called "sleepers", because they remain hidden for years. Some assume false identities and pose as American citizens. They use trickery on others, but manage to keep their distance from some people. There are those who are good actors, and can even marry an innocent American who has no idea she is married to a terrorist. They surface when ordered to attack the enemy. They are ambitious to accomplish their missions and will not allow anyone to stand in their way including their family.

They are in disguise with false I.D.s. Some of them could easily have jobs on cruise ships. Many of these cruise ships belong to American companies; others belong to people in other nations. These terrorist can disguise themselves so their idealistic-suicidal missions can destroy lives at sea or at the harbors where they are docked. All cargo arriving from other countries needs to be searched. Unfortunately, there are not enough inspectors to do this.

Gas companies should check out thoroughly everyone who works for them, especially those whose jobs take them out in the field. Explosions with gas lines is a way they can do harm to Americans. Also people who work on cruise ships, like in the boiler room – they could have phony passports and false names. These terrorists could sabotage airplanes and ships. They could hide explosives inside toys, sporting equipment, and other things that are in the cargo part of a cruise ship or an airplane. As time goes by the military and law enforcement officers will discover them. The terrorists will be arrested and imprisoned; some will be killed by their suicidal mission, or by the military, policemen and other who defy them.

According to the horoscope of the USA, these terrorists masquerade as laborers and are likely to work at airports (especially if a jet crashes due to mechanical failure that was pure neglect). But was it a terrorist who purposely neglected it? Perhaps a terrorist works in the oil industry, motion picture field, or on the floor of the stock exchange, or is employed in stadiums or places where large crowds gather, such as amusement or theme parks. They could hold jobs in these areas, just waiting for orders to do their evil deeds. They were found taking lessons at aviation training schools. They could be employed in hospitals as janitors, security need to be escalated – I.D.s should be thoroughly checked. They could work in bars, cafeterias, restaurants, drug stores in a menial occupation. These terrorists could drop poisonous gas through dust croppers and other type of planes.

These terrorists seek their own personal aim without regard to others. They want to turn the world upside down and destroy those masses of people who they call the "enemy." They use the latest technology to keep in touch with their cell-network of fellow terrorists. Tactics and schemes are well planned and carried out.

These terrorists are cold-blooded, serious, composed, and lack emotional feelings of warmth – they are detached and are determined to carry out their duties. They suppress their hatred feelings for Americans with an icy exterior. They are sly and use devious methods to destroy their enemy. They lack sympathy, and can torment others unmercifully. Self-destruction is part of their plan, regardless of how violent it is. They are cool, keep a low profile and go unnoticed as they tend to their chores.

The FBI and CIA are actively engaged in investigating and tracking down, the network of terrorists and their cells (links). These spies, secret agents and terrorists that live among us will be hunted down by the FBI, CIA, Interpol, and other law-enforcement agencies. Wiretapping, undercover work and going underground is employed by the police, special service operatives, FBI, CIA and armed forces – they could use bugging devices, rockets, and special weapons to track them down and destroy them.

The teamwork with various groups (FBI, CIA, Delta Force, Navy Seals, Green Berets, Rangers and Homeland Security) is prestigious and extremely helpful for our people and government. They enhance the credit and reputation of the USA. Foreign seas are involved when our navy and army go aboard (they work as a team and obey orders). Television, in the United States and overseas gives lots of coverage and bears good news when our attacks on the terrorists are successful. Navy ships could be targeted, however, our hi-tech surveillance systems on these ships are used. The weapons used are the latest in technology. Our troops take action and the special ops units wipe out terrorists and prevent attacks. In for some time and escalating to March 23, 2013, favorable publicity by the press, from those who protect this country and destroy our enemies, is in the news. The President gets credit and the USA's influence in world affairs is enhanced, especially when Osama Bin Laden was killed.

****

In Now and escalating very strong from January 24, 2015 – April 26, 2016

Extra military needs to be employed to prevent attacks by our enemies. This is a highly dangerous time for Americans, especially those who serve in the armed forces.

****

In Now and for the Upcoming Years

Military training increases as people are contacted to serve their country. There is lots of activity for the armed forces, organized labor, and the working people in general. Americans are protected against terrorists and nations who oppose their interest. When the military goes overseas, many Americans will band together in a brotherhood of spiritual harmony (regardless of religion), and are generous with their time and money. Americans rise to the occasion to help those nations who need goods, food – they send relief to those countries in need. Our citizens, who are being held prisoner in some countries, will get some help from the administration.

****

In to February 4, 2013

The new changes and concepts by President Obama bring good luck and change to the American people. The media will give floods of news involving these changes. The USA's business with other nations, who approve of these innovative ideas, enhances our reputation.

However, there are many Americans who will rebel, especially those who prefer the old method of doing business. These activists cause irritations to other citizens and a headache for the administration – in now to January 13, 2013 and October 24, 2013 to September 18, 2014. This action employed by these radicals will in the news causing a stir in the government. But will not be heeded or paid attention to.

****

April 24, 2013 – April 23, 2014

The radical element will be in the news. The people are disappointed with the government and will tend to rebel. They stir things up and want to change the government and get rid of the current administration and put others in power. The courts and their rulings are also in the news – missile and nuclear information is leaked. Committees are formed and meetings held with the Chief of Staffs, Heads of State and Department of Defense – people will try to cooperate (and some will); however, this is a time of shocks and upheavals with those in high places.

The politicians can initiate upsets with sudden changes that lead to exposés. The unusual methods employed make the American public rebel. Legislators and Congressional Representatives are urged by the people to make changes for the improvement of housing and nursing homes. Protests cause upsets and injuries to many. Change is needed but the way-out radical ideas are disapproved by the majority of people, because they are too unconventional and erratic.

Sudden, new and unpredictable changes which bring a marked change from old conditions cause the people to engage in racial activities. It weakens the USA's business and influence in world affairs. The government's honor and reputation is at stake. The issues will involve the people, air pollution, space programs, legislators, congressional representatives and the President. Behind the scenes, secret meetings will be leaked, exposés make sensational headlines. Also, at stake are scientific experiments, health care, prisons, and all places where people are confined. Lots of shocks from every side, from the President and his staff, to the common people. Any newfangled ideas, and way-out change proposed at this time will cause major upheavals in this country. Many Americans will not want to go along with these radical changes. It affects their personal lives, health and routine.

****

In Now and for the Upcoming Years and Escalating to February 9, 2026

Nursing homes for those who are ill, and especially senior citizens, continue to get attention, but much is kept behind the scenes and no one, especially the administration does anything about it. Cut-backs on health care are in the news, and not always correct. But it will make many people rise up in anger. Strife is attracted with those who protest. Some action by the general populace pays off with good results. People could get ill from pesticides in their food; hospitals can be full with patients. Mistakes are made with wrong medication, thus many get ill. Sanitary and other measures could be taken to protect the public's health – there are delays for it to come about. Pharmaceutical drugs cost plenty and many lives are taken from their use. Class action law suits are inaugurated. Congress is slow with new rules and regulations. Spoiled meat, some canned goods, eggs and diseased farm-raised salmon fish could cost lives or make some individuals sick; however the recall of these products is swift, which helps the populace.

There are more and more Americans who seek prevention medicine to improve their health. They can go on strict diets and refrain from eating food that is detrimental to their well being; however, there always will be those who have a disregard for sticking to a regime. Many have found alternative methods of healing such as the Cancer Centers of America. Health care receives a lot of publicity.

The public fight over small animals that are used for scientific experiments; strife is attracted when people become angered over the rights of animals being violated. Many diseases are solved, or helped, in the laboratory; however, it takes years to experiment, and is kept secret until the public is able to benefit from the use of these medicines because the Food and Drug Administration has to research, investigate and approve everything! Americans want measures of protection to insure safety to their children in areas such as school, playgrounds, amusement centers, especially with the food served in school cafeterias. The public wants to be safe when they dine out or eat fast food while attending sporting events. There are not enough inspectors to keep up with the investigations needed. All of these actions cost the government more than they can afford during this time; however, if, and when, the administration obliges the public, the National Debt becomes quite heavy.

There are delays which have senior citizens worried, especially Medicare, Medicaid, insurance and other health programs. Even though there are delays to solve these financial problems, in the long run some benefit will be gained by those who are patient.

Hospitals, rehab centers, nursing homes and all health care facilities will continue to be overcrowded. There are not enough doctors and nurses to care of everyone, especially this will be noticeable once Obama care is effective. It will benefit many, and save lives, with those who before could not afford insurance. However, the influx of patients will cause all of these health care places including hospitals, to be on overload. And that is when it will be noticeable of the shortage of doctors and nurse. This will be in the news, especially from April 24, 2013 to September 18, 2014. The radical element will be busy exposing the bad conditions and service given to the health care of those who are ill. They will shout, "Reform! Break the rules! Change is needed!" Up to October 2, 2018, some administrators and the President will listen and try to do something about it. However, so many disruptions follow that many times these areas will be put on hold. There are fluctuations between regulations and rules being changed to everything being delayed and at a standstill. Then once those with a fighting spirit speak up, sparks fly, action is temporarily taken and then it is back to life in the same rut. Patience is needed.

WAR INTERNATIONAL DISPUTES AND FOREIGN NATIONS

In Now and for the Upcoming Years and Escalating to March 16, 2013

Many foreign allies approve the action taken by our military in the war on our open enemies, especially when Osama Bin laden was eliminated. Other leaders were destroyed by the Navy Seals working undercover for years. Many Americans are relieved that the troops are coming home – and those that have returned from active duty in Iraq. During this time, the ending of wars seems to be closing. However, there can be an increase of outrage by the people of the USA, especially strong from January 25, 2015 to April 26, 2016. War could break out during this time. A few may approve of the action for our involvement, but anti-war protests will be heard by those who are angry that we are at, or may go to, war. There are many Americans who want to fight and defend their homeland and that of other countries. It is a mixed camp, and the war zones could have a high toll due to the attacks on our military forces, resulting in injuries or death.

****

In Now and for the Upcoming Years and Escalating to July 15, 2013

There are iIrritations, and criticism, about the money spent on the war. Behind the scenes, meetings take place with the legislature, and congress. Our ambassadors need to be careful of secret enemies who could become open enemies. They need to guard against being overly confident when stationed overseas. The parties they are host to could be attended by people who they should not trust. Much criticism of this expensive spending will be on deaf ears --- expect more and more spending.

****

In Now and for the Upcoming Years and Escalating to August 3, 2013

The allies we have could go out of their way to help the USA, even though this show-front is a huge expense to the USA. The administration could believe this wanton spending of money is the way to go. It pays off some, but not as much as expected – our hopes are too high. Because of this entertaining there are many favorable financial transactions, including treaties between the USA and foreign nations. All of this entertaining is somewhat good for business overseas and helps our influence in world affairs. Many Americans will be proud because these countries respect us. Although many will disagree, especially Congress. During this time, plenty of money is spent on the war. Many disagreements occur between the President and Congress, especially regarding the funds that the administration feels it needs to allot. No expense is spared by the government on ships that go overseas, or the lavish expenditures spent on foreign embassies. Our ambassadors who reside abroad are treated well by other nations – favors are granted. All of this spending could receive bad press during this time. Members of

Congress could have conflicting views about how the problem can be solved. Aggravations occur because the legislature is trying to find better ways of handling this situation. The current regime is optimistic and tries to instill confidence in the people that we will win the war. The President's speeches are numerous – the press overflows with news that is sometimes distorted. The President is overly confident during this time with his decision; however, Congress and he may not agree on expenditures or treaties with foreign nations. Public opinion polls rate the President badly about how he is handling the war and economy.

Natural resources may be at risk but Congress delays making laws concerning them due to conflicts between members of the Senate and House of Representatives to come to the same conclusion. Congress may want to take measures to change the immigration laws, so that American laborers can be protected from illegal immigrants who take jobs from their citizens. However, there could be postponements to take action because they are unsure of which way to move on this problem. Instead, they may impose tariffs on imported goods, but that may not boost the economy as much as needed.

Matters involving the borders (Mexico, Canada) have to be resolved – thus, congress has to make decisions along these lines. The public may get irritated because there's lots of talk – no action – or there is a disagreement between the administration and members of Congress.

Congress may allot enormous sums of money for the war, thereby increasing the money spent on the military and relief work. The wages of the navy and armed forces could be raised gradually through the years. Many citizens will be deeply divided over the cost of military spending. Protestors, especially from April 24, 2013 to April 23, 2014, might spark violent reprisals. The cost is high to maintain troops in countries we are at war with, or tying to aid the citizens of those countries. Congress may approve of more navy ships and airplanes for the military which puts a drain on American's monetary supply.

Congress may openly discuss reinstating the draft, or there could be breaking news of growing numbers of the armed forces going AWOL. Members of Congress could be divided when it comes to more money to be spent on the war. They may be indecisive about revoking, repealing or acting upon legislative measures during this time. In until September 21, 2016, more women will join the military.

The arbitration between countries, which is placing of differences before some judiciary body to decide (like the United Nations or NATO) will not be so easy. During this time of confusion, misunderstandings and misinterpretations abound; documents may have errors or not be signed. There is much talk and indecisiveness between foreign leaders and the president. The press does not report things correctly. People involved are aggravated as they try to find a better way to solve their problems and differences. Even agreements to do with war, or treaties, present a problem with communication for everyone involved.

****

June 18, 2014 – May 31, 2015

This is an opportune time for President Obama to discuss business with foreign nations, especially neighboring countries. Good decisions can be made with immigration and or borders. Transportation can be beneficial for all concerned. However, there will be some Americans who will criticize his talks. Documents could be signed; publicity for the most part is helpful to the President. Changes can be inaugurated that will benefit all concerned.

****

In Now and for the Upcoming Years; However the worst period is
from January 24, 2015 – April 26, 2016

The USA has been in wars for years. However, it can escalate from January 24, 2015 to April 26, 2016. Americans will be angry if we go to war. Arguments and fights break out. Strife, violence and accidents will be at an all time high. The Department of defense and military will be turned upside down with constant problems and conflicts by the citizens of the USA. Foreign nations, international disputes, threat of war and our open enemies cause difficulties. Americans versus foreigners – Americans want to rush in one moment and not fight the next. They are hot-headed, impulsive, rash, headstrong, assertive and aggressive. They are irritated by their open enemies as well as fighting among themselves. Prisons are overloaded. Abuses and torture to Americans who have been captured increases. The borders need strict security, especially from May 14, 2014, to March 29, 2015. Before any clashes occur, secret enemies can cross the borders and go into hiding – these are mainly spies – because the USA horoscope does NOT indicate terrorists attacking us. We have, in our horoscope, lucky factor that deals with terrorists whether its bombs, nuclear or biological warfare. Our technology is the best anyone can have. In the USA horoscope we have many aspects that indicate we will win. However, our lands (buildings, hotels, private property) have to be protected at all times, but mainly from December 5, 2015 to December 4, 2016.

****

December 5, 2015 – December 4, 2016

The President and the administration receive bad publicity. They have many obstacles in their path involving the heads of government (Presidents, premiers, prime ministers, anyone in an official capacity and in high office). The egos clash – stubbornness reigns. In the USA horoscope we have a lucky aspect involving war that is in now until September 21, 2016 – it implies we will be victorious.

****

In Now and for the Upcoming Years

However, patience is needed. Foreign nations, especially Third World Countries, are slow in paying their debt to the USA. This has been on-going and continues for years. There's a further deficit in the budget, if the government loans money to other countries. They show poor judgment and could put American citizens into a financial panic or slump. The lack of certain raw goods could affect commerce and overseas trading. International commerce might be at a slowdown pace, or at a temporary standstill. Restrictions could be placed upon shipping goods aboard and receiving merchandise that's imported. Tariffs imposed upon foreign goods increase American's revenue. However, some laborers are protected, but the outsourcing we do is hurting the economy of the USA. People are laid off of work or illegals come in and do the job Americans could do. May citizens of the USA refuse to work for low wages, so illegals will gladly take the jobs.

Strict laws that can suspend commerce involving foreign nations are imposed by congress. Tariffs paid on goods imported from cheap labor aboard keep American citizens unemployed, but helps the national bank.

However there could be delays and postponements on hearings; therefore, it may be a long time before the courts make new rulings along these lines. There is a slowdown in the American market of goods exported overseas which could put many Americans on the unemployment line. War and international disputes continue and are slow in being resolved. No wonder its call a "slow war." There will always be open enemies in every country in the world we are not the only nation who has them, but Americans will always stand up and fight for freedom.

Meetings with NATO, the United Nations and other groups, especially involving finances are beneficial to the USA. Allies come to America's aid, especially when we are at war. There is cooperation and teamwork between various groups; the meetings are optimistic and for the welfare of the common people. Committees are formed who work for the good of others; they are specialists who have the responsibility to decide what will benefit the masses and how to obtain the best for everyone. Nuclear treaties could be agreed upon by our allies; however, it is difficult to win over the open enemy in these matters – but not impossible. Nuclear treaties, which involve various groups and agencies from our country and overseas, can be mutually agreed on. There is a delay aspect in, which started years ago, and will continue for years – this is with allies and the open enemy. Some of these open enemies do not trust us or our allies; therefore, they stall and postpone meeting or refuse to arbitrate anything. These leaders tend to be greedy, fearful and ultra conservative and can withdraw from conferences.

Most of the time, the American people cooperate with the government so as to aid the FBI and CIA – that includes Americans living overseas. The FBI and the CIA, most of the time, are successful in arresting many terrorist. Interpol and Law Enforcement groups in various nations will cooperate with the USA.

Many foreign nations know they can depend upon the American government. To them, and to us, it's business as usual. The USA's credit is good with other countries. In world and business affairs our nation is actively engaged in many areas. However there are times when Congress could block the President's efforts, which affects our business ventures with foreign nations.

The President and his cabinet work hard and long hours they seriously try to improve the credit and reputation of the USA in business and world affairs. There will be many people who will disagree and protest the war. When decisions are made, it could be too long in coming; therefore, the economy and American people do not get the boost needed. However, there are some favorable aspects that can help offset the financial problems of the USA and the dealings we have with those oversea nations.

TRANSPORTATION

In to March 23, 2013

There are times when the public can benefit financially with transportation issues. The roads and bridges that need construction and rebuilding could be accomplished easily. The budget can be good. Talks of improving the railway systems, if pushed now could begin. More parking lots could be built. Money spent on construction equipment and materials could be discussed and action could be taken. Issues may be resolved by the Department of Highways and Public Transportation. These agencies can take aggressive action and give good news to the President, the American people and those in Canada and Mexico; discussions that are calm, but where the initiative is taken and pushed. Progress is made and reported. When this occurs, the public is relaxed and is content with the good news they hear from the media.

The military could make the American people feel safe. The Department of Defense, armed forces and police rally together to make our borders safe. Their ideas and actions benefit us as well as the neighboring countries. The press reports favorably along these lines, especially when contracts/documents are drawn regarding our borders. This improves transportation problems as well as benefitting Mexico and Canada.

****

In to August 3, 2013

Transportation prices, (car, bus, trains trucks, toll roads) can increase substantially. The Department of Highways and Public Transportation will issue confusing statements. Misunderstandings can occur with these departments because they may have difficulty getting their ideas across to those who can help bring change. The populace does not always agree with the President's decisions. The press will have a field day with that. The USA's influence in world affairs, also, gets some bad press, especially involving our transportation system. Railroads, cars, motor busses and all modes of transporting goods and people are in the news. Truckers attract problems when carrying goods, especially near the borders of Mexico and Canada.

The borders are in the news; not all the reporters will tell the truth. Confusion reigns with immigration laws; reports are mixed and the public doesn't know who to believe. The Department of Immigration inaugurates changes which the legislatures disagree with. "Change" everyone cries. These lawmakers are overly confident that everything will improve. The borders need more security and stricter regulation, because illegals and terrorists can easily slip through. Some will travel in cars, trucks, by foot or use small aircraft. Their papers are false but they are confident they'll get across without any difficulty. During this time there is an increase of illegal border crossings. Congress could be busy studying these areas for legislative reasons. They could have mixed reports, confusion with what they are told at hearings, plus the newspapers cause things to be stirred up and over exaggerated. Treaties are discussed but not everyone can agree; although there are a few who will try to make headway with their views. The Senate and House of Representatives also differ in their views – thus, causing uncertainty to the American people. The public may get irritated because there's lots of talk – no action – or there is a disagreement between the administration and members of Congress. This not only involves illegals but hearings are also about the railroad system, local airplane traffic, busses, the commercial exchange of goods between neighboring countries, the roads, highways and bridges. Huge amounts of money could be spent during this time. Practicality has been deserted.

****

November 22, 2013 – November 21, 2014

People are aggravated with the President and his administration for not giving enough attention to the transportation system in this country. Better railroads, highways, toll roads, and expressways are on the mind of all Americans, including President Obama. However, due to the press misquoting information it is difficult for the public to believe that officials and the political powers are trying to do anything. The problems worsen with floods, tornados, hurricanes and the people losing their homes, money and possessions. Confusion, misunderstandings and an indecisive administration throws citizens of the USA into panic. The press reports one thing and the administration states something else. Therefore, people don't know where they stand and their income is drained. Everyone knows the National Debt is high and just seems to not get any better – so the public thinks and the press reports.

Shortages occur due to bad weather which affects the crops and grain stored. Labor is costly but the farmer attracts losses rather than gains. Some may not be able to afford the prices the truckers receive from transporting food. This in turn affects the public who lacks the funds to pay higher prices.

****

May 3, 2014 – March 29, 2015

Transportation problems occur when people travel to and from their job. This affects their income, and when toll roads are high, it makes them think about alternate methods. Old roads, freeways, may be taken – or can't because they are in need of repair. If toll prices are increased, the media will give it lots of publicity, thus throwing the public into an emotional tizzy of indecisiveness about their travel vehicles and money spent while not only going to work but also on a pleasure trip. Americans may not want to spend the money to travel for enjoyment or to visit relatives. Obstacles with the National Parks could, also, be an issue with vacationers.

This puts their social, and personal, life on hold – or a strain on their income. Disappointments with trips to Mexico ensue, because people are afraid of danger across the border.

****

June 18, 2014 – May 31, 2015

There is an improvement with all modes of land transportation, thus bringing people chances to travel to neighboring countries as well as cities and states in their vicinity. This gets good press from the media; the President is quoted, or talks about the changes that are being inaugurated with the borders and roads, transportation areas. Many calm down with this news and know they just have to be patient. President Obama is trying to make the correct decisions that deals with trucks, cars, motorcycles, trains and our borders. Documents can be discussed and agreed upon and signed. All of this action opens up new opportunities that can benefit Americans.

****

December 15, 2012 – January 14, 2013; December 5, 2015 – January 5, 2016;
September 20 – October 20, 2016

Transportation prices could skyrocket, but those who travel short distances or to neighboring countries have an "I don't care" attitude. The consumer pays plenty for tickets on trains, toll roads, parking lots, busses, motorcycles, automobiles, and bicycles. Local airplane traffic is increased in price. Excess is in. The public, who does care about higher prices, gives in and feels there is nothing they can do about it.

****

March 7 – April 19, 2013; July 22 – August 21, 2013;
July 25 – August 27, 2014; October 26 – November 26, 2014;
September 15 – October 16, 2015; November 30, 2015 – January 2, 2016;
August 9 – November 30, 2016

Families tend to be emotional. The public may not agree with some of the tactics applied by the administration and bad publicity for the President can occur. People are upset with some transportation issues as well as food prices, the water resources and the fishing industry. Aggravations on how to settle these problems are solved when existing conditions are broken up to pave the way for effort along new avenues of endeavor. This affects the people's income, but there are moments when the general populace is in a good mood involving transportation and makes the best of everything that occurs along these lines, especially March 7 to April 19, 2013.

****

March 17 – April 17, 2013; June 1 – July 2, 2013;
June 23 – September 15, 2013; September 6, 2014 – October 7, 2014;
September 19 – October 19, 2015; December 10, 2015 – January 10, 2016;
December 12, 2016 – January 11, 2017

The preceding dates highlight the aspect in now and, which escalates to September 21, 2016. Action is taken to try to overcome problems with the transportation systems. New roads, bridges are built and rail lines could be extended. Those who manufacture goods, especially food products, benefit because they take the initiative to do something about the methods in which food and retail items are transported. They also do something by pushing, aggressively, products which go to neighboring countries, like Mexico or Canada. Action is taken for the truckers about our borders. They have to fight to get what they want, but are fearless even though disagreements occur and tempers fly. The military could be called in, some of the time, to remedy situations that appear like violence may take place. However, tensions and strife can be expected from neighboring countries, those citizens who reside along the border as well as the various states where goods are transported. In the long run, they are successful. Americans are fighters and rise to the challenge in case of conflict. President Obama, during these dates, is also going to battle with others to get his way, so he can help everyone involved – truckers, the public and neighboring countries.

****

February 8 – May 3, 2013; June 9 – September 2, 2013;
November 10 – December 11, 2013; January 23, 2016 – February 23, 2016;
May 16 – June 15, 2016

Cars, trucks and local airplane traffic between Mexico and the USA could carry illegals and drugs. During these dates some of the smuggling goes undetected. However, October 21- November 21, 2014 and February 14 – March 17, 2015, drugs and illegals could be caught and be in the news – it could be a big bust at this time. Promises made, by the administration to take care of the problems with those cars, trucks and local airplanes that carry drugs and illegals, are blown up and exaggerated. The transportation of legal and as well as illegal goods, or people, brings many disappointments. The public could restrain from crossing borders because they can imagine they will come to harm. Those in the drug business, or users of drugs, will be disillusioned when those they buy from are caught.

****

May 30 – June 29, 2013; March 26 – April 26, 2016

Good news for the truckers and those who drive across the borders for pleasure. The press reports information that is beneficial; perhaps papers, or agreements, are made that helps the consumer as well as those who make a living driving tow trucks or carriers that bring goods to the stores. However, from September 18 – October 19, 2013, and November 15 – December 16, 2015, problems and obstacles ensue; it could be with roads, bridges, trains, cars, trucks and detours or routes that are changed. Perhaps, it is with the administration and bad communications transpiring with neighboring countries. The word of others is misinterpreted and the media misquotes President Obama; thus, confusion with the public and those who drive for a living. Also, papers may not be signed, because no one can agree on the conditions involved between the USA and Mexico or Canada.

****

April 15 – July 9, 2013; June 13 – July 13, 2014; November 9, 2014 – February 9, 2015;
June 5 – July 5, 2015; September 3 – October 4, 2016
December 12, 2016 – January 11, 2017

Local traffic in general has delays and many restrictions, especially with bridges and on the roads. Construction causes delays, debts, and transportation problems. Renovation to make bridges safer and more secure could cost the country plenty. Rules, laws, and regulations laid down to the transportation industry (trucks, busses, railroads) can be delayed in the courts; if passed during this time, heavy tariffs could place a strain in these areas; thus, many people (including truckers) could be unemployed. Truckers lose money when agricultural products, lumber, steel, coal and food are scarce.

People are afraid to travel; the media could report the stricter security is needed to protect the people. Many Americans are fearful of traveling to neighboring countries or overseas. The borders could be closed; careful scrutiny and search is made to those who crass over from Mexico and Canada.

****

June 5 – July 5, 2015; December 12, 2016 – January 11, 2017

During this time people feel safe on roads, bridges, trains and in their cars, especially crossing the borders. Some restrictions are lifted. Delays with roads and detours previously experienced by truckers are improved. The Food prices may be less expensive for the consumer.

****

July 5 – August 14, 2013; August 31 – October 1, 2013

The TSA could bring out new technology that makes it easier to travel as well as more pleasant than it has been. Cars, trucks, trains and all motor vehicles could contain the latest computer devices that improve driving. However, there are recalls on some of these items or problems that ensue. Roads could be changed, problems with the weather could have highways and various roads washed out – anything could happen. It is the unpredictable that a driver needs to expect; radical changes which make the consumer rebel. People will want, and some will, to break the rules. It is an erratic period for President Obama, his administration and the citizens of the USA as well as Canada and Mexico. Many shocks which are upsetting – it could be that lightening hits a tree that blocks roads or a bridge suddenly caves in.

****

July 22 – August 25, 2013

Conflicts with people who want to take a vacation – should they travel and spend the money it costs with tolls and gas or should they stay home? Some National Parks could be closed, thus causing those who want to go to them to be disappointed. However, threw are many enjoyable moments spent on travel from May 18 – June 18, 2014 and December 14, 2014 to March 30, 2015. Those who want to attend art exhibits, musical ventures, picnics, social events, or go to the national parks or a resort for a vacation – they feel they can afford various forms of entertainment. These are the people who have good jobs, or income, and do not worry about money.

****

August 9 – September 12, 2013; July 3 – August 2, 2016

Aggravations grow between the average person and the President and his administration. Those in power, and who have authority, could create difficulties for the populace. The areas involved could be with transportation, bordering countries, trucks that carry goods to the stores, and food supplies. Bad weather could be the cause or a hurricane or earthquake. People may not have food in their homes because of a catastrophe. They may be upset because they feel that FEMA, other officials, and the President have not given them the attention and care they need.

****

January 14 – February 14, 2014; March 7 – April 6, 2014

Obstacles occur with trucks carrying nuclear devices. Crusades against the carriers driving through towns will be in the press. Terrorists could cross the borders and destroy the masses. Bombs could be on busses and other modes of transportation such as trains. Rail tracks need to be inspected. Enforcement of tight security checks are needed on trains and busses. Chemicals and waste products could have spills on the roads, thus causing these highways to be closed. TV and reporters could be in the news daily with all the problems Americans are facing. Borders could be closed, thus, affecting the income and work of a trucker and all mail systems. The people working, that give service to others, need to be investigated, thus making sure they are not spies or terrorists. The criminal element, at borders, could carry so many illegals and drugs across, that Americans protest daily. The news on radio, television or the internet will be full of all of these activities. The average person will believe the President and his administration is doing a poor job.

****

September 1, 2014 – October 3, 2014; June 22 – July 23, 2015

The truckers, cab drivers, and the people who drive motor vehicles to work are in good spirits. They take pleasure crossing borders to Mexico, Canada or to neighboring cities and states. Their confidences could stem from President Obama signing treaties with Mexico that could benefit everyone. Thus, the public spends lots of money on transportation – their own cars or on toll roads. President Obama, and his administration, is given very favorable reports by the press. It seems to be a happy time for the consumer, vacationers and President.

****

December 27, 2014 – January 29, 2015; April 2 – May 3, 2015

The public and those in official positions attract good luck with the borders, transportation, money, the roads, and bridges. The housing conditions may have some improvement, thus people can travel to their homes, and farms. Produce, and other goods the truckers carry, are not overly priced and the consumer and farmer are all in good spirits.

****

May 10 – June 9, 2015; June 19 – July 22, 2016

The President could receive bad publicity for activities involving the borders or transportation problems of the worker (those who are in road or bridge construction). This affects the public and their money. If tolls are too high, or bus and train fares are on the rise, the consumer will complain. The press will have a field day with all of this commotion that is transpiring.

****

July 21 – August 20, 2016; September 11 – October 11, 2016

There is improvement for the citizens of the USA regarding mass transit, especially bullet trains that are safe and secure due to special devices that have been attached. Also, new trains will be comfortable and attractive; thus, people will enjoy spending their money on this mode of transportation. Short journeys and vacations will be on the rise. There are important developments in transportation. Meetings are held by various transportation agencies; those involved are cooperative. The public is willing to go along with their solutions.

American people may express their opinions on television, radio shows and the internet regarding transportation. There is teamwork with various factions who want to do well for the

USA. Success comes through broadcasting, advertisements and books that are published relative to trains, highways, freeways, roads, bridges and airplane traffic. People travel to conventions which flourish. Enormous crowds fill the convention halls. However, this is not an overnight improvement – it is a gradual, little-by-little pick up of business.

EDUCATION, COMMUNICATION AND THE MEDIA

In Now and escalating until March 23, 2013

The press has a field day when the President receives outstanding recognition. Thus his reputation, and that of the USA, receives favorable publicity. This increases the risk-players on Wall Street to forge ahead. America's influence in transportation areas, with neighboring countries, is enhanced. The education system ideas expressed by President Obama are received favorably by others. Action is taken, employment picks up, especially for teachers, mechanics and those in the health care fields. The public is receptive to some of the news covered by the press, especially interviews regarding schools, colleges, education and telecommunications. The attention the government gives toward a child's future, and all young people, are reported by the media. Thus, the people of the USA are happy that the President is taking action along these lines. There are beneficial changes instrumented in these areas and the field of communications. Those in these various industries, including manufacturing, aggressively push toward change, which results in good luck for the country.

****

In Now and escalating until August 3, 2013

Even though the press and people are content with some of the ideas expressed by President Obama, there are others who do not see the same picture.

The communications industry experiences many changes which are not to the people's liking. The airwaves buzz with lots of activity; interviews and speeches are continually being given by the President and his staff. Misinterpretations, and out of context reporting is done by the Media. The Press has a field day: newspapers, magazines and television coverage are non-ending – gossip prevails. White House reporters and leaders of other nations can be misquoted. There are many changes bandied about for Education with confusion and decisions getting bad publicity. The Department of Education as well as postal representatives gives conflicting news. The Media could slip up and make a blunder on their reporting; thus, people become more upset when they discover these inaccuracies. There is indecision regarding the postal prices: are they going to be increased?

Postal prices may increase. The post office is losing money because the majority of people use e-mail, UPS or FedEx instead of the postal services. It is likely that the higher prices raised at this time is bad judgment on the part of the postal authorities. The Press doesn't let up for one minute reporting the news as it comes in; however, some information is speculative and misinformation could leak into the coverage the reporters are doing regarding Education and the new laws Congress is debating over in this area. This bad publicity stirs up the public and is not helpful to the USA's influence in World Affairs. Law makers are overly confident and tend to overlook some details that are needed. Many Americans now, more than ever, use cell phones and send faxes. There is lots of talk of an overloaded phone system. Satellite Communication systems are increased and cost an enormous amount of money which causes the public to voice their opinions against everything. Money spent on the education of children, schools and colleges is exorbitant, especially that allotted by Congress who is excessive with the spending of money. Different views could be broadcast by commentators, politicians and the government. The public may air their views – the media could be flooded with misinformation expressed by those in, and out, of power.

The press is busy reporting confusing news – much talk by the media continues to escalate on a daily basis. The administration is withholding war information from the press, but somehow the reporters still write confusing articles that appear in periodicals, newspapers, magazines and are aired on the radio and television. The leakage from the administration to the media serves just that purpose – after all, if the facts were all told about what the government is doing that would be an aid to the terrorists.

America's ambassadors entertain lavishly, because they want favors from other nations and could be overly confident they will be obtained. There are times when the bad press reports outweigh the good. The Red Cross and others receive attention regarding their humanitarian efforts but may not receive all that they hope for.

****

May 3, 2014 – March 29, 2015

The literacy rate of many people receives bad press, especially those who cannot read or write English – like those from neighboring countries such as Mexico. Confusion and indecision reign involving the borders and educating people. This is costly to the people of the USA. Much talk is done along these lines and the press does not let up a minute. The President is trying to solve this problem but gets slack on its cost from the people as reported by the media. The news is filled daily with this bad publicity. Many believe that those from neighboring countries are taking the easy way out and not trying to learn – that reflects on the President which keeps the newspapers and news media in business. Books for the education of others, many believe, are a waste of money because people do not take them seriously. The teachers are not plentiful and do not receive the money they deserve, thus more confusion is created which the press reports. The Department of Education as well as the Department of Roads, Highways and Public Transportation are brought into play during this time. It is a difficult time for President Obama who is trying to initiate change only to have all of these departments, the media and the American people throw obstacles in his pathway.

****

June 18, 2014 – May 31, 2015

Many discussions with foreign nations at this time bring favorable publicity to President Obama. He is making change that is favorable to the USA and prevents war or international disputes with other countries. Opportunities for changes with neighboring countries, transportation systems, the borders and illegals could be beneficial to everyone. Documents may be signed that are helpful to everyone concerned; however, the press reports mixed opinions – some criticize his ideas, other are all for them.

****

In Now and for the Upcoming Years

The government, as reported by the press, may discuss the need for Americans to economize. Statistics indicate that the USA is at an all-time low in earning capacity, taxation, collecting money from those who owe our country, and government spending. When can Americans expect relief? These are up and down periods for years to come. The problem could be that the administration is receiving lots of publicity about solving the nation's business outlook, but Congress could block the President's efforts.

Cell phones will be buzzing with non-stop talk. New telephone systems, using satellites, are installed which can link up to cell phones world-wide. These phones, and systems, could be as easy as calling anyone in the same city – without a sim card or special phone call to hook up internationally. The manufacturing of these new cell phones will be bought like hot cakes. This could help the stock market in these areas. The mail is flooded with junk mail and informative letters which keep Americans alert to the latest technology. Radio and TV commercials, ads in magazines, newspapers and the internet will be prominent and increase the income of a large body of people. The tabloids will flourish with juicy gossip about the celebrities, especially those who endorse the new phone systems.

Art, music, the National Parks, fashion, cosmetics, and lavish parties are in the news. Auctions gain enormous press because of the exorbitant money spent on paintings, jewelry, coins, objects d' art.

The Department of Treasury releases favorable news to the American people. Finances, for many, especially the wealthy, increases. Weddings of celebrities are in the news telling about how much was spent when a couple tied the knot. The press has a field day reporting these elaborate receptions and the wedding gifts. Those who work in any of these artistic-related areas will enjoy a boost to their finances.

The world-wide news coverage coming from the USA can be misinterpreted by foreign nations. Thus, misunderstandings can occur due to the press reporting events, as well as, the administration talking or giving information in a way that causes us to have problems with other nations, even our allies. The President is very visible giving many pep-up speeches over the radio and television as well as increasing his press conferences. Excess is the name of the game with the President's overly confident attitude. He tries to encourage the public that everything is improving, and in some areas, he is correct.

News involving senior citizens gets printed: their pensions, Medicare, Social Security, and insurance/health care programs. People may worry about laws being passed which could cause them to have reduced checks, or health care problems. This type of action, reported by the media has the seniors nervous and confused. Conflicting reports due to misquotes or mistakes are made…delays, postponements wind up being the talk of the day.

The press echoes the cry of conservationists and environmentalists to conserve the natural resources and environment for the children of the future. There are delays with the courts for solving these problems, although some rule may be imposed making many products prohibitive. Many Americans are depressed with this news and concerned; however, the media does report conflicting opinions. Such as one moment capitalism is helping people, therefore the people should not be afraid to spend their money; the next moment telling people that the recession is in and therefore everyone needs to cut down on costs and save their money.

ENTERTAINMENT

In to March 23, 2013

Lots of activity in the sports areas – arenas, stadiums, colleges, universities, race tracks and games of chance. The casinos do well, especially with those who are risk-takers. Many Americans think of gambling as entertaining; however, when they lose they may change their tune. There are those involved in these areas that, up to February 4, 2026, are conservative – those are the type that are bad losers. Those who enjoy and thrive on leaping in fast to the challenges of betting have an attitude of "win some, lose some." These sporty types need to learn caution from January 24, 2015, to April 26, 2016 – that is not the best time for sports events or taking chances. USA citizens could be torn with making choices. During this period, they will be angry with themselves for their risk-taking betting. Also, during this time athletes need to avoid injuries. The people of the USA tend to be fighters and will jump in to all sorts of conflicts from January 24, 2015 to April 26, 2016 – in fact more so than in the past. Many entertaining sports events hold disappointments, and bring out people's temper, because they or their favorite athlete lost. There are others, who will laugh it off and control their rage. Sports events and casinos can be in the news very strong – mixed publicity (for and against certain players or casinos) up to December 20, 2014. In until February 4, 2026, action is taken by Americans to aid the armed forces, those hurt in battle, hospitalized veterans and the needy – the action is entertainment to raise money. Celebrities, especially sports stars, will go behind the scenes to rehab centers and hospitals to entertain the troops spending time there. Many will travel overseas to perform for them. The press will report all of the good being done by those who entertain others for a worthy cause.

Sporting events (boxing, wrestling, tennis, football, baseball, etc.) will attract huge crowds who are willing to spend lots of money for tickets. Arenas and stadiums will be filled, although there are many who will spend their money for an event by watching TV. These frugal types, who are interested in sports, will hesitate spending too much. However, there are some that will at the last minute go on a small spree. Some sporting events lose money, especially with those athletes who command huge salaries. But other types of action events will bring their owners enormous sums of money – capitalism shows up even in sporting events.

****

In to August 3, 2013

The public will spend lots of money on entertainment, such as shows that will make them laugh – stand-up comedy in nightclubs, comedic films and TV sitcoms. The critics will have a field day reporting mixed reviews of these various shows and performers. Religious and philosophical films or plays will, also, be popular.

Ticket prices will increase substantially. In fact, there will be lots of ticket-gauging and some people may not think the show was worth the price paid. All amusement centers and theme parks are overly confident and send prices spiraling. The movie industry will spend more money to make a film than ever before. Broadway shows will be costly for the investor. Everyone thinks prices will soar. Those who have money have an "I don't care what it costs" attitude. During this time casinos will thrive with more customers who are willing to take a chance on big bucks. The same goes for those who play the lottery. These forms of taking a risk will aid the lucky ones in their search for wealth. The tax revenues from casinos, and the states (lottery players), help boost the economy. Many gamblers will risk everything they have during these dates. The unemployed will be careful with taking a chance on winning anything. They are cool-headed conservatives who don't take risks – they calculate everything they do and pinch pennies.

****

November 22, 2013 – November 21, 2014

When the President spends lots of money on entertaining in the White House – dignitaries, royalty, celebrities, prime ministers and presidents of other countries as well as VIP's in the USA, the press will give bad publicity mainly due to the amounts spent. This will be especially strong with those from Canada or Mexico. Agents and agencies involving the borders could visit the White House and the cost could aggravate Americans. However from June 18, 2014 to May 31, 2015, the press could give coverage to the President and his entertaining that will be favorable. American, Canadian and Mexican citizens could applaud President Obama, not only for the entertaining, but for the results obtained. Talks will help everyone. His ideas bring many opportunities to everyone involved.

****

May 3, 2014 – March 29, 2015

Society people, designers and artists could spend lavishly on galas, benefits, shows and art exhibits. The money spent creates an obstacle with the common people, and the press is right there to report it. News stories in magazines and newspapers, especially gossip columns, will aid the various charitable causes they cater to. Cocktail parties abound with lots of idle chit-chat; their designer clothes and jewels will be mentioned by those who attend – the press or their friends. Art exhibits with their champagne parties will keep the rich hobnobbing among themselves; many will spend lots of money on a painting or object d' art.

Even though these parties upset many Americans, there are others who entertain lavishly in their homes or treating their friends to lunch, dinner and all sorts of parties. Therefore many are confused as to "should they entertain or not?" Going to movies may be all the entertainment some people want and they consider that a good escape and not hard on their bank account. This is in until May 19, 2013 and from November 10, 2015 – September 28, 2016. During this time Americans will enjoy spending their money on their children's entertainment – amusement and theme parks, movies, water shows, the zoo and games. These areas of business can make money, but not as much as anticipated.

****

In to February 5, 2017

Although people desire to escape into the world of fantasy, their pocketbooks restrain them from spending. Another aspect has been in, and will be in, for years which indicate that the public has to sacrifice fun in order to eat and survive due to a bad economy – many are unemployed. However, there are a few who will take a risk and spend hastily on movies and worry about the consequences later. Movie stars, and stage stars, give of their time to perform for charitable causes. Musicals on the screen and stage, as well as industrial shows, tend to thrive; however, the backers take a greater risk than anyone because they do not earn the big sums expected.

Films will receive lots of publicity, especially up to September 15, 2014. However, some critics of theatre and movies will not be so kind to those involved in the production. But the box offices will still make money. As they say in the entertainment field, "Bad publicity is better than none!" From November 22, 2016 to February 19, 2018, the movie industry, theme parks and amusement parks can have many disappointed consumers who may not frequent them as much as they did in the past.

Entertainment complexes such as arenas, stadiums, amusement centers, theme parks, theaters, night clubs and movie houses could be surrounded by heavy security. Many Americans could be afraid to go to these places because they are fearful of bodily harm, especially if the press reports that the public needs to be aware of danger – this type of publicity is in now and escalates to February 5, 2017.

****

December 15, 2012 – January 14, 2013

The public spends, spends and spends on entertainment, fun, pleasure, sports and having the time of their lives. Cost means nothing to many. The movie theatres and sports arenas could be packed. Broadway show ticket prices could be exorbitant but no one's seems to care, except those who are unemployed and frugal. The populace wants their children and loved ones to enjoy as much as possible in the realm of entertainment. Box office sales soar.

****

March 7, 2013 – April 19, 2013; May 30 – June 29, 2013; July 22 – August 21. 2013

    The public gets restless for change: fluctuations between the common people and the President to look for better ways of handling issues receives lots of publicity from the press. Mood swings prevail and a large number of people could be affected by the changes that are made, especially when it comes to entertainment. However, the American people, especially women, enjoy entertaining and being entertained. Families will get together, such as going on picnics, having friends over for barbecues or attending concerts. The May 30 to June 29, 2013 period gives favorable publicity to the President and his family – the enjoyments and pleasures they encounter as well as how they are entertained just like the average person receives.

****

In until September 21, 2016; March 17 – April 17, 2013;
June 1 – July 2, 2013; June 23 – September 25, 2013

    The entertainment industry and sporting events receive both good and bad publicity. The public and the administration are restless. The USA's influence in world affairs gets lots of press, thus causing President Obama's views to fluctuate. However, Americans will always be in the news. The publicity escalates in the sports and entertainment fields.

    The public will be more aggressive during this time; in fact, some of them could be fearless and go out in public places without any harm coming to them. They will have a great time playing sports or entering tournaments or marathon races. These types are aggressive, physical, gutsy, nervy and courageous. However, the police, armed forces and Department of Defense come to the rescue of those who think they are in danger while on a vacation, or at a sporting event or entertainment complex. Good luck abounds between the common people and the military or police.

****

April 15 – July 9, 2013

    There are some delays and postponements with shows, sporting events and openings. The public is somewhat fearful of going out in public and attending entertaining events. Those who are not afraid may refrain from enjoying the pleasures of life, because they do not have or do not want to spend their money. However, there are moments when there is a safe feeling, as well as a small boost in the economy.

****

May 30 – June 29, 2013

The press, including critics, will give favorable reviews for all types of entertainment; parties, theater, movie, sporting events, theme parks and amusement centers. The masses can enjoy themselves, especially if something is of an intellectual nature. It is a favorable time for sporting events to make headlines, and large-quick-easy bucks. Games and stars in the field shine brightly bringing good fortune to all involved.

****

July 5 – August 4, 2013; August 31 – September 12, 2013

Many radicals will be in the limelight rebelling against the sports and entertainment fields. Upsets will affect many, including the administration and President Obama – however, good luck will eventually shine through all the turmoil. Strikes could affect the theaters, arenas and stadiums – it could be with the transportation fields, however, it could be due to sudden events affecting the homes of many Americans. It could be hurricanes, floods and other disasters are at the root of the problem. Entertainment areas could be shut down, possibly people in those areas will rebel and not come to work. The President will get some bad press for his involvement, or non-involvement, but in the long run he will not have his reputation damaged. And the public will calm down.

****

July 16 – August 16, 2013

Even though conditions are bad involving citizens of the USA, the President or entertainment fields, many shows and theatres will be affected. The populace will still flock to the theatres and the Movie and Theatrical Industry will make some money. Everything is not as bad it seems.

****

July 22 – August 25, 2013

The artistic, fashion and cosmetic world as well as art exhibits and parties could be costly and lose money for these people. Food prices could skyrocket thus causing many to cancel social engagements. If the President gives a lavish party at this time, the press received will not fare well with anyone. Galas, banquets and the society, artistic and average person's world will be in turmoil. The average person and the society element do not seem to get along and those who are employed, or serve (like in restaurants) the wealthy may not be treated properly. Thus, restaurants could lose money and establishments that cater or do weddings could also have revenue upsets. Art galleries who host parties may not attract many people, and they could attract losses of money spent on parties they had planned.

****

August 9 – September 12, 2013

There are aggravations between the public and the administration. President Obama could receive bad publicity, especially when he entertains politicians, prime ministers, and VIP's. The money spent, the public and press could complain, should be on the homeless and shelters. Hurricanes could cause problems so that the President cannot entertain those in power. It could cause many issues with the general populace and officials – anyone in power, especially over financial aid. Thus, the entertaining that the President does is not approved by others who are powerless to do anything about the issue that is taking place.

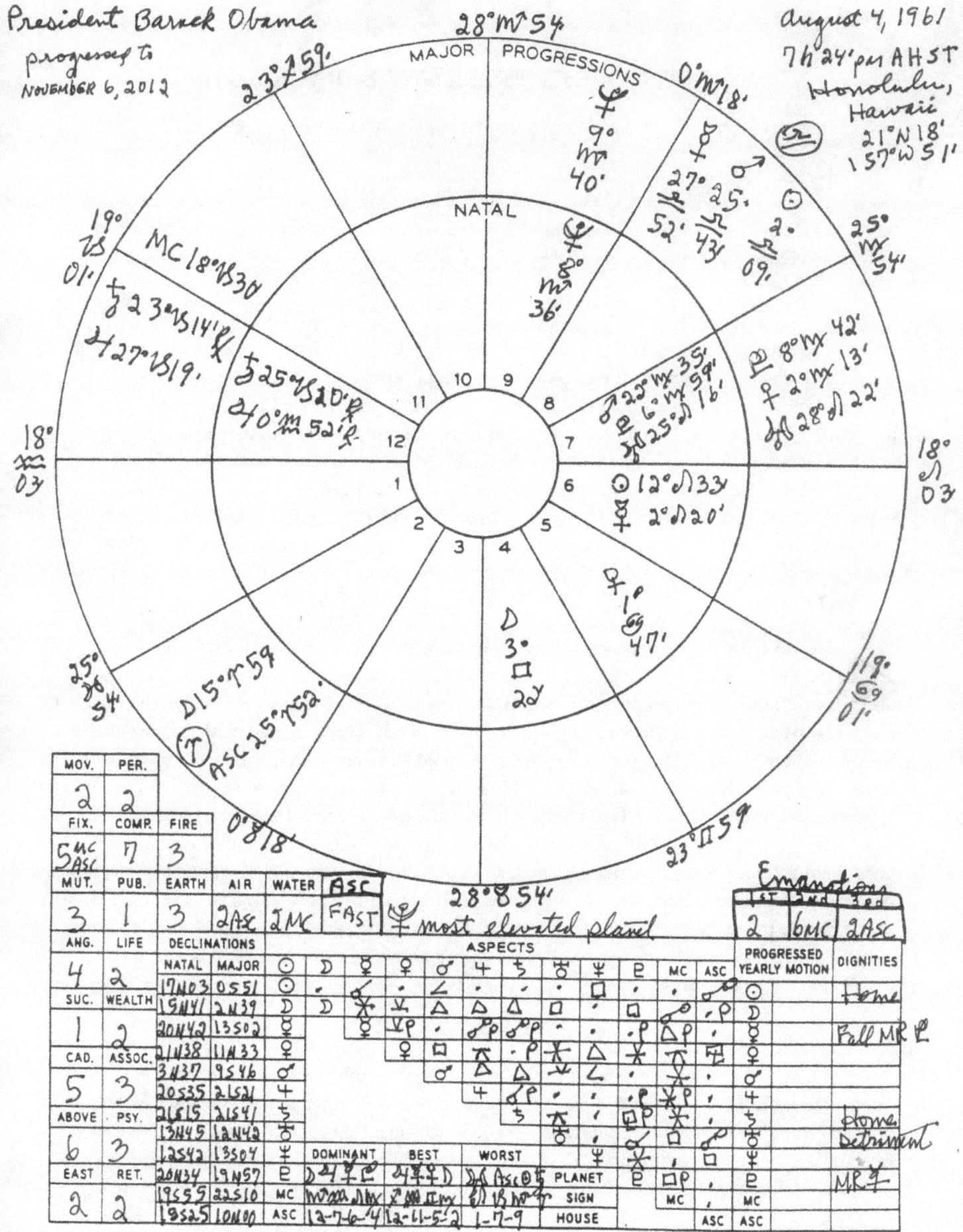

THE HOROSCOPE OF PRESIDENT BARACK OBAMA

In now to April 28, 2013 and thereafter will remain in his horoscope for years.

President Obama is a humanitarian and very idealistic. He wants better conditions for the world. He may not realize he is intuitive and psychic about his beliefs. Often, he may be quiet while he is busy contemplating these ideals. He is secretive and driven to obtain his desires. He is disappointed when they don't materialize.

January 20, 2013 – January 28, 2014

The President is proud of his staff and works very hard to achieve his goals. He is able to understand, and be in touch, with the common classes of people as well as the powerful – leaders, dignitaries, royalty, officials and those in high positions. He will work for the good of the people. Luck will be with him when he tries to get others to work with him, especially about taxes and deals with other people's money, insurance, Medicare and many of those on his staff can praise him. He will also pat them on the back for doing a great job. There will many important conferences with prime ministers, presidents and VIP's as well as government and administrative workers. Some people will respond favorably to his being commander in chief and able to be a good leader. They understand that his actions are because he wants to do the best job that he can.

However, he has aggravations that lead to conflicts with congress and important leaders around the globe. And in the horoscope of the USA, it is indicated that the President would have obstacles with these same people – that is until January 1, 2013. However, in his own chart, these aggravations and conflicts are in until October 6, 2013. These are ego clashes – he wants his way, is stubborn, and may not get everything desired. The problems stem from dealing with taxes, other people's money, insurance, and Medicare. It is an ego clash – he is stubborn and so are they. However, he will try to be charming and explain both sides of the coin. President Obama has weighed the pros and cons but some members of Congress will create obstacles and he will not get his way on everything he wants. Therefore, even though he has good aspects, this powerfully discordant one could cause obstacles. Perhaps, he will be a little adaptable, once he thinks clearly to see the other person's side as well as his. Once this aspect is gone, he does not attract this type of obstacle in the future. Hopefully, it won't take that long until issues are decided upon by both parties.

In to May 3, 2013

There are sudden opportunities from foreigners, government workers and those in his immediate staff. He is ingrained to make decisions that he feels right about. He may weigh the pros and cons, but he is intuitive this time. President Obama wants peace, equality, democracy, freedom and fair play for everyone. The press responds favorable to his ideas. Interviews will increase. Before making any decision, he will think about it and the impact it will make on others. However, he may not realize that a quick decision, during this time, stems from intuition. Unexpected events transpire with work, sudden changes take effect – issues he has been working on for a long time. He is intelligent and is able to express his views readily. These decisions will involve his job, staff, congress and the tax situation, insurance, health care, Medicare, foreign nations, the automobile industry and going green. These are some of his humanitarian ideas that he wants to bring about – and he can at this time. He has many other decisions for the entire time he is in office. Favorable publicity will result, especially as October 22, 2013 approaches. There will always be some delays with these issues and with his efforts to inaugurate change, but he has a mind that doesn't stop. He worries about everything – his ideas, the people's money-taxes. However, these concerns are when he is alone and behind closed doors. Often negotiations are slow. But he is patient, serious and dedicated to take care of his responsibilities.

September 3, 2015 – September 20, 2016

There is good luck with the president expressing his views – his charm will win over many people. The social scene, and tending to business at the same time, will benefit his talks and deals he makes with his staff, strangers, travels to other countries, and those in power that can aid his beliefs. Documents can be signed and treaties, those especially with transportation issues, immigration and borders. Travel to neighboring countries will be beneficial – great progress will be made. He is kind to those who work for him. He has warmth, which is not always shown, but will be more so during this period. People are receptive to him. Issues are solved regarding taxes, insurance, Medicare and deals with other people's money. However, the money spent on travel and entertaining can be plenty, but it pays off.

March 14 – December 21, 2013

There is an increase of secret activities going on behind closed doors; deals with our spies, secret service, undercover agencies, refuges and investigations. It could have to do with charitable institutions or those who have been taken prisoners by our enemies. Negotiations that are kept from the press can take place. However, he is too confident and may have some disappointments if things don't materialize.

October 2, 2013 – April 8, 2015

He has to guard against impulsive action in regards to negotiations behind closed doors, and issues involving the people's money, insurance taxes, Medicare, the military and spending (he could want to give the military a raise). He is in a hurry to accomplish his aims. He may want to initiate, another stimulus plan for the unemployed. Or give aid to the poor refuges overseas. Obstacles could occur, but he won't let anything stop him. President Obama will be aggressive and fight in the behalf of the needy. He will want to get grants for those going to college. He may be interviewed by the media and talk about people donating to charitable institutions. He is an enormous spending mood (for the good of others). His own money is not as important to him as helping those who don't have anything. He will push for higher taxes for the wealthy – some people will approve and others will create obstacles. However he is relentless and will struggle and fight to get laws changed or passed.

In until October 30, 2017, but much stronger from May 17, 2015 – May 23, 2016

Obstacles and aggravations occur when he meets with various groups of people --- such as the FBI, CIA, unions, corporations and those who are open enemies. The terrorists, and their destruction, will be uppermost on his agenda. Osama Bin Laden was destroyed under this same aspect. President Obama is not content with stopping one terrorist, but he will want to have covert operatives go after all of them. Undercover and secretive meetings take place. There will be people, who at meetings will be uncooperative with him, but this is an obsession with him and he will be in the news for his actions along these lines. Many will protest on television and the internet. There will be masses of people who will create obstacles in his pathway. His known enemies will continue to investigate him. They are out to ruin his reputation and career. They could try to force him to resign. The press and internet (various websites) will have a field day with trying to destroy him. However, it will backfire, because his favorable career and reputation aspects outweigh anything discordant.

During this time, the USA horoscope has aspects for serious problems with our open enemies. It could be war, or the people fighting over foreign disputes. However, during some of this time, President Obama has difficulties at meetings with groups of people, NATO, the United Nations and dictators. It may be that he will receive a lot of bad publicity over terrorists or his meeting with open enemies. Sneaky activities could occur with these various associations. Others may not want to join forces with the USA. It is a drastic change aspect and places groups against each other. It could be one group breaks up another rival group and no one agrees on anything. It is force, pressure and demands made. President Obama will not yield to these destructive groups. They could try to get him to do something illegal or against his desires and principles. He will not be cooperative and will have difficulty getting others to cooperate with him.

However with all of the preceding that could occur, President Obama has favorable aspects with his reputation, although he has some damage if he gets too controlling or forceful. His favorable reputation aspects are in for years – it is his confidence and secret negotiations behind closed doors which helps him. His military actions and careful planning are in for years. These are taken very seriously, and when he feels he is doing the right thing, he will push fast and accomplish tremendous tasks. He is a very responsible person and takes his duties seriously and is cautious and security conscious. He will delay everything until it is time to be aggressive. The President is a diplomatic person and does everything in a slow and determined fashion. Delays with negotiations could be strong from March 13, 2016 to September 5, 2016. He can keep quiet about his plans. He has favorable publicity thru July 25, 2017. He could have some aggravating press from March 13, 2016 to June 24, 2016. However, he has more harmonious publicity in years to come than he does inharmonious.

December 9, 2015 – October 4, 2016

President Obama can have a league of nations, such as NATO, the United Nations or other groups meet with him. Progress can be made with open enemies and terrorists. These conferences could involve allies and others who believe in his idea of a better world for the universe. Teamwork and a cooperative effort is the result. Socializing with these various groups, and turning on his charm and analytical ability, will be outstanding. He demonstrates a caring and nurturing attitude to those who are in power as well as the downtrodden – the underdog. His credit rating can soar. Many members of the press, and those who have websites, will give him outstanding recognition for his efforts for peace. He could receive a humanitarian award.

July 6, 2015 – February 14, 2017

Sudden and aggressive action will take place which involve the military, raises for those in our armed forces, and spending on the latest technology for our defense system. Modern, new inventions will spring up and the moment President Obama hears about them – he will leap in. He will be actively engaged in foreign issues, international trade and commerce, manufacturing companies in the USA and infrastructure. Building, and all sorts of construction – all new concepts will be innovated rapidly. This quick action will bring many opportunities for the good of humanity. New ideas with taxes, insurance, Medicare, fundraising and pensions for people could be in the news and be successful. New laws could be passed for the benefit of everyone. President Obama will be extremely busy traveling overseas. Relations with people aboard bring many opportunities for foreign transaction and there could be more companies from overseas that move their business to the United States and employ Americans. The world court favors him and the press speaks highly of his actions. Trips, and events, transpire suddenly without prior notice – like lightening flashing. New inventions help others and he will push to acquire them for our manufacturing concerns that will also use the latest technology. Computer businesses could move to the USA.

March 27, 2016 – April 25, 2017

President Obama could get confused, do repetitious thinking and have great difficulty rendering decisions regarding documents, foreign trade or travel, and speaking before the masses. He could have obstacles with his staff, because he is indecisive. Communication with others can create problems in his working environment. His conflicts become strong starting June 15, 2016 and make it even more troublesome to make decisions. He is torn in various directions – like being on a see saw. The president could think about writing about his job as President. It is a nervous condition that can also cause insomnia. He could be trying to make up his mind as to what he will do when he leaves office. It is confusion which is not part of his nature. Thus, this mental experience throws him for a loop, as well as causes misunderstandings with his staff and misquotes by the press.

September 29, 2016 – October 5, 2017

There is teamwork and cooperation with his staff and various groups. A small opportunity could be attracted as far as a future job is concerned. People in power, dignitaries and world leaders meet with him. The courts favor him. His efforts to do good deeds for the masses get favorable publicity. Appearances on television or lectures bring opportunities, especially when he is no long the president of the USA. Colleges and universities could pay him for speaking at their various functions. An advance for writing a book could be substantial and good for his ego. Overseas trips can be advantageous – he has made many good contacts with VIP's and influential people.

July 12, 2016 and in to the Upcoming Years

Many trips could fall through. Disappointments prevail with the promises others make. Lies and deceptions could occur. He may not see himself as he is in reality. A desire to escape could make him plan a trip to some remote place, but it may not happen. His imagination is active. He needs to rest and go to a wellness spa and recover from all the stress the presidency has given him. President Obama may procrastinate in writing and may seem absentminded. He needs to avoid getting lazy, while still in office and work hard and keep so busy that he does not have time to dwell on the lies, deceptions or disappointments others bring him. His good aspect for hard working and keeping his nose to the grindstone is in for years. It has always been his luck factor for success.

www.ingramcontent.com/pod-product-compliance
Lightning Source LLC
Chambersburg PA
CBHW080349170426
43194CB00014B/2736